PIERRE ELLIOTT TRUDEAU

PIERRE ELLIOTT TRUDEAU

Thomas Butson

1986
CHELSEA HOUSE PUBLISHERS
NEW YORK
NEW HAVEN   PHILADELPHIA

SENIOR EDITOR: William P. Hansen
PROJECT EDITOR: Marian W. Taylor
ASSOCIATE EDITOR: John Haney
EDITORIAL COORDINATOR: Karyn Gullen Browne
EDITORIAL STAFF: Maria Behan
        Pierre Hauser
        Perry Scott King
        Kathleen McDermott
        Howard Ratner
        Alma Rodriguez-Sokol
        John W. Selfridge
ART DIRECTOR: Susan Lusk
LAYOUT: Irene Friedman
ART ASSISTANTS: Noreen Lamb
        Carol McDougall
        Victoria Tomaselli
PICTURE RESEARCH: Matthew Miller

First Printing

Library of Congress Cataloging in Publication Data

Butson, Thomas G. PIERRE TRUDEAU.

(World leaders past & present)
Bibliography: p.
Includes index.
   1. Trudeau, Pierre Elliott. 2. Prime ministers—Canada—Biography.
I. Title. II. Series.
F1034.3.T7B88 1986   971.064'8'0924 [B] [92]   86-4136

ISBN 0-87754-445-X

Chelsea House Publishers
Harold Steinberg, Chairman and Publisher
Susan Lusk, Vice President
A Division of Chelsea House Educational Communications, Inc.

133 Christopher Street, New York, NY 10014

345 Whitney Avenue, New Haven, CT 06510

5014 West Chester Pike, Edgemont, PA 19028

Contents

ADENAUER	FRANCO	MARY, QUEEN OF SCOTS
ALEXANDER THE GREAT	FREDERICK THE GREAT	GOLDA MEIR
MARK ANTONY	INDIRA GANDHI	METTERNICH
KING ARTHUR	GANDHI	MUSSOLINI
KEMAL ATATÜRK	GARIBALDI	NAPOLEON
CLEMENT ATTLEE	GENGHIS KHAN	NASSER
BEGIN	GLADSTONE	NEHRU
BEN-GURION	HAMMARSKJÖLD	NERO
BISMARCK	HENRY VIII	NICHOLAS II
LEON BLUM	HENRY OF NAVARRE	NIXON
BOLÍVAR	HINDENBURG	NKRUMAH
CESARE BORGIA	HITLER	PERICLES
BRANDT	HO CHI MINH	PERÓN
BREZHNEV	KING HUSSEIN	QADDAFI
CAESAR	IVAN THE TERRIBLE	ROBESPIERRE
CALVIN	ANDREW JACKSON	ELEANOR ROOSEVELT
CASTRO	JEFFERSON	FDR
CATHERINE THE GREAT	JOAN OF ARC	THEODORE ROOSEVELT
CHARLEMAGNE	POPE JOHN XXIII	SADAT
CHIANG KAI-SHEK	LYNDON JOHNSON	STALIN
CHURCHILL	BENITO JUÁREZ	SUN YAT-SEN
CLEMENCEAU	JFK	TAMERLAINE
CLEOPATRA	KENYATTA	THATCHER
CORTÉS	KHOMEINI	TITO
CROMWELL	KHRUSHCHEV	TROTSKY
DANTON	MARTIN LUTHER KING, JR.	TRUDEAU
DE GAULLE	KISSINGER	TRUMAN
DE VALERA	LENIN	QUEEN VICTORIA
DISRAELI	LINCOLN	WASHINGTON
EISENHOWER	LLOYD GEORGE	CHAIM WEIZMANN
ELEANOR OF AQUITAINE	LOUIS XIV	WOODROW WILSON
QUEEN ELIZABETH I	LUTHER	XERXES
FERDINAND AND ISABELLA	JUDAS MACCABEUS	ZHOU ENLAI
	MAO	

ON LEADERSHIP
Arthur M. Schlesinger, jr.

LEADERSHIP, it may be said, is really what makes the world go round. Love no doubt smooths the passage; but love is a private transaction between consenting adults. Leadership is a public transaction with history. The idea of leadership affirms the capacity of individuals to move, inspire and mobilize masses of people so that they act together in pursuit of an end. Sometimes leadership serves good purposes, sometimes bad; but whether the end is benign or evil, great leaders are those men and women who leave their personal stamp on history.

Now, the very concept of leadership implies the proposition that individuals can make a difference. This proposition has never been universally accepted. From classical times to the present day, eminent thinkers have regarded individuals as no more than the agents and pawns of larger forces, whether the gods and goddesses of the ancient world or, in the modern era, race, class, nation, the dialectic, the will of the people, the spirit of the times, history itself. Against such forces, the individual dwindles into insignificance.

So contends the thesis of historical determinism. Tolstoy's great novel *War and Peace* offers a famous statement of the case. Why, Tolstoy asked, did millions of men in the Napoleonic wars, denying their human feelings and their common sense, move back and forth across Europe slaughtering their fellows? "The war," Tolstoy answered, "was bound to happen simply because it was bound to happen." All prior history predetermined it. As for leaders, they, Tolstoy said, "are but the labels that serve to give a name to an end and, like labels, they have the least possible connection with the event." The greater the leader, "the more conspicuous the inevitability and the predestination of every act he commits." The leader, said Tolstoy, is "the slave of history."

Determinism takes many forms. Marxism is the determinism of class, Nazism the determinism of race. But the idea of men and women as the slaves of history runs athwart the deepest human instincts. Rigid determinism abolishes the idea of human freedom—the assumption of free choice that underlies every move we make, every word we speak, every thought we think. It abolishes the idea of human responsibility, since it is manifestly unfair to reward or punish people for actions that are by definition beyond their control. No one can live consistently by any deterministic creed. The Marxist states prove this themselves by their extreme susceptibility to the cult of leadership.

More than that, history refutes the idea that individuals make no difference. In December 1931 a British politician crossing Park Avenue in New York City between 76th and 77th Streets around ten-thirty at night looked in the wrong direction and was knocked down by an automobile—a moment, he later recalled, of a man aghast, a world aglare: "I do not understand why I was not broken like an eggshell or squashed like a gooseberry." Fourteen months later an American politician, sitting in an open car in Miami, Florida, was fired on by an assassin; the man beside him was hit. Those who believe that individuals make no difference to history might well ponder whether the next two decades would have been the same had Mario Contasini's car killed Winston Churchill in 1931 and Giuseppe Zangara's bullet killed Franklin Roosevelt in 1933. Suppose, in addition, that Adolf Hitler had been killed in the street fighting during the Munich *Putsch* of 1923 and that Lenin had died of typhus during the First World War. What would the 20th century be like now?

For better or for worse, individuals do make a difference. "The notion that a people can run itself and its affairs anonymously," wrote the philosopher William James, "is now well known to be the silliest of absurdities. Mankind does nothing save through initiatives on the part of inventors, great or small, and imitation by the rest of us—these are the sole factors in human progress. Individuals of genius show the way, and set the patterns, which common people then adopt and follow."

Leadership, James suggests, means leadership in thought as well as in action. In the long run, leaders in thought may well make the greater difference to the world. But, as Woodrow Wilson once said, "Those only are leaders of men, in the general eye, who lead in action. . . . It is at their hands that new thought gets its translation into the crude language of deeds." Leaders in thought often invent in solitude and obscurity, leaving to later generations the tasks of imitation. Leaders in action—the leaders portrayed in this series—have to be effective in their own time.

And they cannot be effective by themselves. They must act in response to the rhythms of their age. Their genius must be adapted, in a phrase of William James's, "to the receptivities of the moment." Leaders are useless without followers. "There goes the mob," said the French politician hearing a clamor in the streets. "I am their leader. I must follow them." Great leaders turn the inchoate emotions of the mob to purposes of their own. They seize on the opportunities of their time, the hopes, fears, frustrations, crises, potentialities.

They succeed when events have prepared the way for them, when the community is waiting to be aroused, when they can provide the clarifying and organizing ideas. Leadership ignites the circuit between the individual and the mass and thereby alters history.

It may alter history for better or for worse. Leaders have been responsible for the most extravagant follies and most monstrous crimes that have beset suffering humanity. They have also been vital in such gains as humanity has made in individual freedom, religious and racial tolerance, social justice and respect for human rights.

There is no sure way to tell in advance who is going to lead for good and who for evil. But a glance at the gallery of men and women in *World Leaders—Past and Present* suggests some useful tests.

One test is this: do leaders lead by force or by persuasion? By command or by consent? Through most of history leadership was exercised by the divine right of authority. The duty of followers was to defer and to obey. "Theirs not to reason why,/ Theirs but to do and die." On occasion, as with the so-called "enlightened despots" of the 18th century in Europe, absolutist leadership was animated by humane purposes. More often, absolutism nourished the passion for domination, land, gold and conquest and resulted in tyranny.

The great revolution of modern times has been the revolution of equality. The idea that all people should be equal in their legal condition has undermined the old structures of authority, hierarchy and deference. The revolution of equality has had two contrary effects on the nature of leadership. For equality, as Alexis de Tocqueville pointed out in his great study *Democracy in America*, might mean equality in servitude as well as equality in freedom.

"I know of only two methods of establishing equality in the political world," Tocqueville wrote. "Rights must be given to every citizen, or none at all to anyone . . . save one, who is the master of all." There was no middle ground "between the sovereignty of all and the absolute power of one man." In his astonishing prediction of 20th-century totalitarian dictatorship, Tocqueville explained how the revolution of equality could lead to the "*Führerprinzip*" and more terrible absolutism than the world had ever known.

But when rights are given to every citizen and the sovereignty of all is established, the problem of leadership takes a new form, becomes more exacting than ever before. It is easy to issue commands and enforce them by the rope and the stake, the concentration camp and the *gulag.* It is much harder to use argument and achievement to overcome opposition and win consent. The Founding Fathers of the United States understood the difficulty. They believed that history had given them the opportunity to decide, as

Alexander Hamilton wrote in the first Federalist Paper, whether men are indeed capable of basing government on "reflection and choice, or whether they are forever destined to depend . . . on accident and force."

Government by reflection and choice called for a new style of leadership and a new quality of followership. It required leaders to be responsive to popular concerns, and it required followers to be active and informed participants in the process. Democracy does not eliminate emotion from politics; sometimes it fosters demagoguery; but it is confident that, as the greatest of democratic leaders put it, you cannot fool all of the people all of the time. It measures leadership by results and retires those who overreach or falter or fail.

It is true that in the long run despots are measured by results too. But they can postpone the day of judgment, sometimes indefinitely, and in the meantime they can do infinite harm. It is also true that democracy is no guarantee of virtue and intelligence in government, for the voice of the people is not necessarily the voice of God. But democracy, by assuring the rights of opposition, offers built-in resistance to the evils inherent in absolutism. As the theologian Reinhold Niebuhr summed it up, "Man's capacity for justice makes democracy possible, but man's inclination to injustice makes democracy necessary."

A second test for leadership is the end for which power is sought. When leaders have as their goal the supremacy of a master race or the promotion of totalitarian revolution or the acquisition and exploitation of colonies or the protection of greed and privilege or the preservation of personal power, it is likely that their leadership will do little to advance the cause of humanity. When their goal is the abolition of slavery, the liberation of women, the enlargement of opportunity for the poor and powerless, the extension of equal rights to racial minorities, the defense of the freedoms of expression and opposition, it is likely that their leadership will increase the sum of human liberty and welfare.

Leaders have done great harm to the world. They have also conferred great benefits. You will find both sorts in this series. Even "good" leaders must be regarded with a certain wariness. Leaders are not demigods; they put on their trousers one leg after another just like ordinary mortals. No leader is infallible, and every leader needs to be reminded of this at regular intervals. Irreverence irritates leaders but is their salvation. Unquestioning submission corrupts leaders and demeans followers. Making a cult of a leader is always a mistake. Fortunately hero worship generates its own antidote. "Every hero," said Emerson, "becomes a bore at last."

The signal benefit the great leaders confer is to embolden the rest of us to live according to our own best selves, to be active, insistent, and resolute in affirming our own sense of things. For great leaders attest to the reality of human freedom against the supposed inevitabilities of history. And they attest to the wisdom and power that may lie within the most unlikely of us, which is why Abraham Lincoln remains the supreme example of great leadership. A great leader, said Emerson, exhibits new possibilities to all humanity. "We feed on genius. . . . Great men exist that there may be greater men."

Great leaders, in short, justify themselves by emancipating and empowering their followers. So humanity struggles to master its destiny, remembering with Alexis de Tocqueville: "It is true that around every man a fatal circle is traced beyond which he cannot pass; but within the wide verge of that circle he is powerful and free; as it is with man, so with communities."

—New York

1

The Firebrand

On June 24, 1968, a slender, well-dressed man was prepared to address a large and excited crowd in St. Hyacinthe, a town in the predominantly French-speaking Canadian province of Quebec. The man had been greeted with such enthusiasm that a stranger might have assumed a pop superstar had arrived. The figure at center stage, however, was not an actor or a musician. He was the prime minister of Canada, Pierre Elliott Trudeau.

"Our home," Trudeau told his audience, "is not just the province of Quebec. Our home is the whole of Canada." This was the last day of what had been a grueling campaign for the prime minister, and he was showing some signs of fatigue. Still, he spoke with the energy and courage for which he was known, directly confronting the highly charged issue of Quebec's separation from the rest of Canada, which was—and is—predominantly English-speaking. "Let us live united!" he exclaimed.

The speech was a rousing one, but Trudeau was unable to finish it as the crowd roared its approval. He had addressed the people in French as well as English, emphasizing his strong belief in the im-

Prime Minister Pierre Elliott Trudeau (b. 1919) greets Montreal supporters before Canada's June 25, 1968, national elections. Impressed by Trudeau's wit, vitality, and optimism, the voters returned him to office by the largest electoral margin in the nation's history.

AP/WIDE WORLD PHOTOS

CANAPRESS PHOTO SERVICE

A Montreal demonstrator, shouting *"Vive le Québec libre"* (Long live free Quebec), demands independence for the largely French-speaking province. Pierre Trudeau, himself a native Quebecer, strongly opposed the movement to separate Quebec from Canada.

13

Visiting Italy during a 1933 family vacation, 13-year-old Pierre Trudeau acquaints himself with the pigeons of Venice. Trudeau's childhood trips gave him a lifelong passion for foreign travel.

portance of both languages in Canada. As he made his way through the crowd after his speech, Trudeau felt a hand grab at his jacket. He turned and saw a beaming young woman running toward her boyfriend. "I touched him, I touched him!" she shouted.

The son of a French-speaking father and an English-speaking mother, Pierre Trudeau was fluent in both languages. He was educated in Canada, England, France, and the United States. Trudeau was thus well-suited to the task of leading Canada through the difficult period that began in the early 1960s, when some of the French-speaking citizens of Quebec began to advocate secession from the Canadian union.

Few Canadians were neutral about Trudeau during his first campaign for the prime ministership of Canada. Many voters criticized what they felt was his lack of seriousness; they also disapproved of his tendency to be sarcastic when faced with opposition. Many more, however, were delighted with his wit, his personal charm, his wide-ranging education, his skill at sports, his love of adventure. Young people were especially attracted to his refreshing and unconventional style. In 1968 Canada was swept by a new phenomenon: "Trudeaumania."

From his birth on October 18, 1919, Joseph Pierre Yves Elliott Trudeau had been both gifted and privileged. His father, a Montreal lawyer, had owned a chain of 30 prosperous service stations. He sold the chain to a major oil company in 1931 for $1.4 million and, through astute investments, multiplied that amount many times. The Trudeau home was in an affluent part of Montreal. Each morning the family chauffeur drove Pierre to school in a limousine. In the afternoon, the chauffeur came to take him home.

Pierre was Charles-Emile and Grace Trudeau's second child. The first was a daughter, Suzette, who was 18 months old when Pierre was born. A third child, Charles Jr., would arrive later.

Charles-Emile Trudeau was a well-known and popular Montreal figure whose French-Canadian ancestry could be traced back ten generations. The money from the sale of his gas station chain had not all gone into conservative investments; he had also bought an amusement park and a controlling interest in the Montreal Royals baseball team. As a principal farm club of the Brooklyn Dodgers, the Royals would later include on their roster such famous athletes as Jackie Robinson, Roberto Clemente, and Tom Lasorda.

Although he was an exceptionally busy man, Charles-Emile invariably came home every day at 5 P.M. to spend time with his children. It was a practice that Pierre would seek to follow when he had young children of his own. The family spent weekends together hiking and canoeing in the Canadian wilderness. On Sunday evenings they would gather to listen to music.

Later, Pierre would say of his father: "He was a man I admired very much. . . . He had a lot of friends, the house was always full of friends. And he was big in my eyes, but he was obviously big in the eyes of his friends, too. He was a leader, he had

If the politicians didn't take him seriously, the people did. From the day he announced his candidacy to the day the convention opened, he won more headlines and more polls than his competitors put together.
—the *Toronto Daily Star*
June 26, 1968

Unemployed workers in Paris, France, stage a protest march during the Great Depression of the 1930s. The wealthy Trudeau family's 1933 European trip made young Pierre realize that many people faced hardships unknown in his privileged world.

wit . . . he was physically strong." He added, "To me he embodied universal wisdom."

In the spring of 1935, Charles-Emile went to Florida to observe the Royals' spring training. While there, he caught a virus that rapidly brought on pneumonia. Within three days he was dead.

His father's death naturally brought great changes to young Pierre's life. Suddenly, at the age of 15, he was the oldest male in the family. With Charles-Emile gone, Grace Trudeau figured more dominantly in the lives of her children. Just as his father's flair for activism and having a good time undoubtedly rubbed off on young Pierre, his mother's more cautious personality influenced him too.

Grace Trudeau's quiet refinement had been a perfect foil for the robust energy of her gregarious husband. But she was adventurous too, in her own way. She took her young children on canoe trips and later, when Pierre was a university student, she liked to zip around town on the back of his motorcycle. It was probably from Grace that Pierre derived his taste for foreign travel. It had been she who persuaded Charles-Emile to take the whole family to visit Europe in 1933, during the height of the Great Depression. That trip, taken when millions of workers were unemployed and facing poverty, demonstrated to young Pierre just how different his family's life was from those of less fortunate people. Later, Trudeau said that his mother showed him the value of freedom, while his father taught him the value of discipline.

At the age of 12, Pierre entered Jean de Brébeuf College, an elite school run by Jesuits, an order of Roman Catholic priests. It was a fine school that combined a high-school and university-level education for boys and young men. Although most of the students were wealthy, some were the exceptionally bright offspring of poor families. Competition between the two groups was intense. Starting out with basic academic studies, they moved on to philosophy, the arts, and political science.

Trudeau thrived in this atmosphere. Classmates remember him as a student who was always at or near the top of his class academically. But some also

A school portrait of Trudeau in 1938. When he entered Montreal's Jean de Brébeuf College at the age of 12, Trudeau thought of himself as an Anglo-Canadian who spoke French; when he graduated eight years later, his self-image was that of a French Canadian who spoke English.

recall a less admirable side of Trudeau. His reserve in dealing with those he considered inferior, and the acid tongue for which he became known in later life were not assets that won him widespread popularity. The group of similar souls that gathered round him were known by the other students—in that peculiar mixture of French and English known as "franglais"—as "Les Snobs."

At Jean de Brébeuf College—named for a 19th-century French missionary—young Pierre came under the influence of a 25-year-old priest named Robert Bernier. Like Trudeau, Bernier came from an upper middle-class French-Canadian family. In his home province of Manitoba, Bernier's father was a lawyer and a member of the provincial legislature. In later life, Pierre Trudeau would say: "Father Bernier was the most highly cultivated man I had met and he confirms what I am always saying—that you can be a damned good French Canadian outside Quebec. Bernier was the man who talked politics to me. He was my teacher of letters, of French literature. He really taught me to like beautiful things, poetry or books or art; he really set standards of appreciation which have never left me."

Trudeau graduated from Brébeuf with a bachelor of arts degree in 1940. He had a broad background not only in French literature but in the writings of such American authors as Ernest Hemingway, William Faulkner, and Henry James. He was also thoroughly familiar with the works of political philosophers—especially John Locke, Alexis de Tocqueville, and Thomas Jefferson. Young Trudeau's already conservative outlook was reinforced by the atmosphere of the school and the attitude of the students with whom he associated most closely.

By 1940, Canada was embroiled in World War II, a conflict that inspired little enthusiasm in Quebec. Many French-speaking Quebecers saw the war as no more than a British effort to gain world domination, and they strongly resisted being drafted to fight such a war. Trudeau was among the first who actively protested the sending overseas of conscripted men. He campaigned for an antiwar candidate in 1942, but more often than not, his

Pierre Trudeau practices a handstand on a Canadian beach in 1937. Always athletic, the Canadian leader often said the happiest times of his childhood involved "the joys of the forest, the lake, canoeing, swimming, running . . . climbing mountains."

Canadian troops arrive in England during World War II. The conflict, which Canada entered in 1939, sharply divided the nation. In a 1942 vote, 80 percent of the English-speaking electorate favored allowing the government to send draftees overseas; 72 percent of Quebec's French-speaking voters opposed the move.

Trudeau and a fellow student in France mug for the camera in 1946. After obtaining a master's degree from Harvard University, Trudeau studied at the Sorbonne in Paris and at the London (England) School of Economics.

contempt for the war took such forms as long excursions into the country on his Harley-Davidson motorcycle or pranks in which he dressed in a World War I German uniform. These activities eventually earned him expulsion from the Canadian Officers Training Corps (similar to ROTC in the United States). Later commenting on his behavior during this period, Trudeau said, "I think it was sort of to bug the government."

In the fall of 1940, Trudeau enrolled as a law student at the University of Montreal. Removed from the elitist atmosphere that had prevailed at Brébeuf, he came into frequent contact with people from less privileged backgrounds. He began to think about social and economic conditions. "I saw certain friends at the university who had to prepare their exams on the kitchen table with a dozen brothers and sisters around," he said later, "whereas I could work quietly in a room at home. I found it was unjust."

Quebec students protest the sending of conscripted (drafted) men overseas in 1944. Pierre Trudeau, like most French Canadians, regarded conscription as a symbol of British domination of Canada.

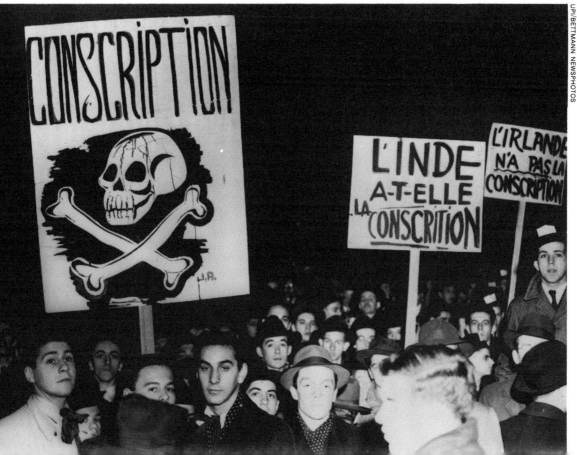

UPI/BETTMANN NEWSPHOTOS

Arab militiamen guard a road position in Beersheeba, Palestine, in 1948. Trudeau, always attracted to high-risk situations, arrived in Palestine in the middle of a full-scale war between Arab countries and the new nation of Israel.

After Trudeau received his law degree in 1943, he signed on as a junior member of a leading Montreal law firm. He thought the work, however, was dull and unrewarding and a year later he abandoned his legal career. In 1945 he entered Harvard University to work toward a master's degree in political economics. Exposure to the rigors of a Harvard graduate school was something of a shock to Trudeau. He had been at the top of his class at both Brébeuf and the University of Montreal. Now he realized that there were serious gaps in his education. In typical fashion, he was determined to fill those gaps; after earning his degree at Harvard, he went to Paris, France, to study at the Ecole des Sciences Politiques and the law school of the Sorbonne.

Trudeau was less than impressed with French schooling. "I had just left Harvard," he said later, "and, in all modesty, I knew more of these subjects than most of my professors [in Paris]." He spent most of the next year following his own course of study and riding around Paris on a motorcycle.

It was during this year in Paris that Trudeau renewed his acquaintance with another young Quebecer, Gérard Pelletier. The meeting led to one of the longest and most important relationships of Trudeau's life. The son of a railroad agent from rural

Citizens of Quebec, do not be content to complain. Enough of patchwork solutions, now is the time for cataclysms.
—PIERRE TRUDEAU
campaigning, during his
law school years, for
anti-draft candidate
Jean Drapeau

Quebec, Pelletier had first met Trudeau while Trudeau was studying at Brébeuf and Pelletier was a pupil at a less elegant school nearby. Both had studied at the University of Montreal, but it was not until their meeting in Paris that a real friendship developed. Pelletier was a shy, retiring young man, while Trudeau was self-assured, sometimes even arrogant. "I liked him, though his flippancy disconcerted me a little," Pelletier said later. Not wealthy like Trudeau, Pelletier earned his living by working for an international student relief agency.

From the beginning, Pelletier was impressed by Trudeau's intellectual capacity and ability to form and support an opinion on almost any political subject. The two engaged in long discussions about Canadian political subjects. These exchanges would, several years later, lead to the establishment by Trudeau and Pelletier of *Cité Libre* (Free City), one of Canada's most influential political magazines.

In 1947, Trudeau left Paris for London. There he enrolled at yet another university, this time the London School of Economics, where he took lectures from Harold Laski, a celebrated socialist political scientist and economist. Trudeau worked much harder at his studies in London than he had in Paris. After a year, he decided to reward himself with a trip around the world. It was the first of several such journeys, all of which were to feature a series of wild escapades and scrapes with authority.

The first trip was a solitary journey, in keeping with the aspect of Trudeau's personality that made

Wearing traditional Middle Eastern garb during his visit to Palestine, Trudeau was arrested by the Arabs as a suspected Israeli spy. "Those travels," he said later, "were alternative ways of accumulating knowledge . . . and, I guess, testing myself."

21

him prefer such individual sports as swimming or skiing to team sports like hockey. Dressed in hiking shorts and an open-necked shirt, carrying the rest of his belongings crammed in a backpack, he trekked from Germany to eastern Europe. He tried to enter Yugoslavia without a visa, but he was promptly jailed and then deported to Bulgaria. There he fell in with a group of Spanish-speaking Jewish refugees with whom he journeyed through Greece and Turkey. In the ancient crossroads city of Istanbul, he followed the example set by the English poet Lord Byron a century earlier by swimming across the Bosporus, the strait that separates Europe from Asia.

From there he moved south to Palestine, which was then the scene of bitter conflict between the Palestinians and the newly arrived Jewish settlers. Trudeau, who by this time had grown a beard and was dressed almost in rags, was arrested and briefly detained by the Arabs as a suspected Jewish spy. From Palestine he moved across the Middle East to Iraq, where he visited the site of the ancient city of Ur. While he was inspecting the ruins there, Trudeau was attacked and captured by bandits. He began to shout nonsense in *joual*, the rural Quebec dialect of French. Deciding he was not only poor but insane, the bandits let him go.

Trudeau continued on, through India and into Burma, where he found himself in the middle of a civil war. The next stage of his journey took him to Indochina, where a war between France and her rebellious colonies was in progress. Somehow he reached China, where yet another war was raging, the epic struggle between the communist forces led by Mao Zedong and the nationalist forces led by Chiang Kai-shek. For a time Trudeau was in some danger but he managed to leave Shanghai on an American troop carrier just as the victorious communist troops entered the port.

Later, Trudeau was to explain the motivation behind his frequent flirtations with danger: "I tempted fate. I used to deliberately put myself into some pretty tricky situations just to see how I would handle them."

All the forbidden places, I try to go to.
—PIERRE TRUDEAU

Physically, Trudeau was equipped for such demanding adventures. He was an ardent swimmer, jogger, and skier; he loved to spend weekends hiking and climbing in the woods, and he was a top-notch diver. Desmond Morris, author of *The Naked Ape*, once remarked that Trudeau had "certain animal leadership properties—as a zoologist, I'm tremendously impressed with Trudeau. He has an intellectual virility which is exceedingly important. . . . His anatomy, his gestures, his facial expressions are animal qualities that set him apart and bring him to the top of the heap."

When asked about his love of physical challenges, Trudeau said, "I like to test my physical and mental limits all the time. I get fun out of a new experience. I like to feel alive. I like to taste new fruit or dive into new waters. This is to me what is good about life. It's making sure that you are using yourself to your limits. That's why I like sports."

A U.S. Navy ship evacuates Americans from Shanghai, China, in 1949. Trudeau, who had arrived in China in the final days of the civil war between the Chinese nationalist and communist forces, escaped Shanghai on a similar ship just as the victorious communists entered the city.

2

Finding a Mission

Trudeau's adventurous lifestyle earned him a reputation as a restless young man, unable to focus on any subject for a sustained period. His way of life on his return to Canada did little to change that impression. On the surface at least, he remained something of a dilettante, a 30-year-old rich boy toying with many activities but seemingly unable to devote anything more than passing attention to any one subject. In addition, the urge to travel was still strong; in the next few years he would frequently disappear from Canada to see what was happening in the far corners of the world.

The year 1949 was a turbulent one in the province of Quebec. The ultraconservative provincial government led by Maurice Duplessis was using all its powers to repress any sign of liberalism, whether in the workplace, the church, or elsewhere.

The focus of opposition to the Duplessis regime had been fixed in the small Quebec mining towns of Asbestos and Thetford Mines. In February 1949, the asbestos miners there went on strike, demanding higher pay, better working conditions, and impartial handling of grievances. The Duplessis government was bitterly opposed to the miners and

UPI/BETTMANN NEWSPHOTOS

Conservative Maurice Duplessis (1890–1959) was premier of Quebec when the province's asbestos miners went on strike in 1949. Outraged by the harsh measures Duplessis employed to crush the strike, Trudeau took up the cause of the beleaguered miners—and thereby began his political career.

Pierre Trudeau strikes a characteristic pose on a Utah ski slope in 1977. During his tension-filled years in office, the Canadian leader found relaxation in strenuous physical activity, particularly in such individual sports as swimming, hiking, skiing, and scuba diving.

AP/WIDE WORLD PHOTOS

25

A miner is arrested during one of the bloody battles that characterized the 1949 strike in Asbestos, Quebec. Trudeau's sympathy with the miners was long-lived; 26 years later, when they were again on strike and he was prime minister of Canada, he sent them a cable expressing his support.

their demands. To agree to them would have undermined the comfortable arrangements the government had with the mine management and with other businessmen throughout the province. Few people, including the miners themselves, were surprised when, in an attempt to break the strike, the government called on the police to disperse demonstrations, escort and guard strikebreakers, beat up isolated miners, and force the strikers to withdraw their picket lines.

Trudeau's friend Gérard Pelletier was by this time a reporter for the French-language newspaper *Le Devoir*. Assigned to cover the strike, he invited Trudeau to drive over to Asbestos with him. When the pair reached Asbestos, the police stopped their car, searched it, and told them in no uncertain terms to get out of town. Undaunted, they stayed on.

Trudeau soon met the strike leader, Jean Marchand, who was basically the opposite of Trudeau and Pelletier in character. Where they tended to be cool, intellectual, and detached, Marchand was quick-tempered, emotional, and deeply committed to his cause.

In ambitions and sympathies, however, the three had much in common. Marchand invited Trudeau to speak to the strikers about their legal rights. The miners, who quickly nicknamed the skinny, straggly bearded city fellow "St. Joseph," were not impressed by the newcomer at first. But Trudeau, whose speech switched from legal matters to a passionate oration about human rights, ended up enthralling his audience. Starting off with his own recent encounter with the provincial police, he recounted for the unsophisticated rural Quebec audience his experiences in repressive foreign police states. The connection was immediately grasped by the strikers.

Another reporter who was there said: "It was quite a thing to see this young man go out and speak to 5,000 miners. It was profoundly moving. I remember his standing in the big hall talking about democracy and liberty in a way they understood right off. He spoke their language."

For the rest of that year, Trudeau remained deeply involved in the cause of the Asbestos miners. He was a frequent visitor to the picket lines, even when the police were making indiscriminate mass arrests. And he worked hard as a lawyer for the union—without pay—until the strike ended in July 1949.

> *It is all too easy, should disturbances erupt, to crush them in the name of law and order. We must never forget that, in the long run, a democracy is judged by the way the majority treats the minority.*
> —PIERRE TRUDEAU

PUBLIC ARCHIVES CANADA

Pierre Trudeau discusses labor issues with Gérard Picard, a Canadian trade union official, in 1957. Trudeau spent most of the 1950s editing the influential political magazine *Cité Libre* and traveling. "You'd write him a letter in Montreal," commented one friend, "and back the answer would come from Sardinia."

Former Canadian Prime Minister Louis St. Laurent (left; 1882–1973) congratulates newly elected Liberal party leader Lester Pearson (1897–1972) in 1957. Although Trudeau had strongly criticized Pearson, particularly on the question of nuclear weapons, the two were to become staunch political allies.

Trudeau's introduction to the fiery Jean Marchand and to the world of strikes and labor politics marked a turning point in his life, setting him on the road that would lead to the nation's highest elective office.

Soon after the settlement of the Asbestos strike, Trudeau went to Ottawa, Canada's capital, where he had been hired as an economic adviser in the Privy Council Office. This was the office from which the prime minister—at the time Louis St. Laurent—gathered his information and pulled the strings by which the government functioned. St. Laurent, a veteran Quebec policitian whose grandfatherly image belied his sharp mind and vigorous disposition, had been swept into office the year before. After a long period in which Anglo-Canadian politicians had dominated political life in Ottawa, a new era had arrived: Canada's central figure could now be a French Canadian.

Trudeau's duties in Ottawa did not occupy all his time. Every weekend he returned to Montreal to talk with Pelletier about the magazine they had dreamed of in Paris. It was to be a publication in which they could present their views on the problems facing Quebec and Canada.

Visiting China in 1960, Trudeau (left) and his old friend, Montreal publisher Jacques Hébert (b. 1923), inspect a section of China's Great Wall. After completing their six-week tour, the two coauthored a tongue-in-cheek travel book, *Deux Innocents en Chine Rouge* (*Two Innocents in Red China*).

Cité Libre finally appeared in June 1950. Although its circulation never exceeded 2,500 copies, it was influential. In defining the magazine's purpose, Trudeau wrote: "We must submit to methodical doubt all of the political categories that the previous generation bequeathed to us: the strategy of resistance is no longer useful for the full flowering of the City. The time has come to . . . throw out the thousand prejudices with which the past burdens the present, and to build for the new man. Let us cast down the totems, break down the taboos. . . . Dispassionately, let us be intelligent."

Pelletier later recalled what he termed the "curious" way in which *Cité Libre* was edited. Each week the principals would meet, usually in Pelletier's home. Potential contributors would read their essays aloud, the assembly would comment, and the piece would be accepted or rejected. The *Cité Libre* gatherings would eventually be expanded into what came to be known as *Le Rassemblement*, a loosely knit discussion group of intellectuals dedicated to reforming the Liberal party and ousting the Duplessis provincial government. In addition to Trudeau, Pelletier, and Marchand, it included René Lévesque and Robert Bourassa, both to become successors to Duplessis as Quebec premier (the leader of a provincial government is called a premier).

There was no doubt that Duplessis was the prin-

A Royal Canadian Air Force BOMARC missile on its North Bay, Ontario, launching pad in 1963. Incensed by Lester Pearson's decision to permit the emplacement of nuclear weapons in Canada, Trudeau labeled the prime minister "the defrocked priest of peace."

Quebec Premier Jean Lesage (1912—80) addresses a Liberal party meeting in 1962. Although Trudeau agreed with his fellow Quebecer's policies on education and welfare, he strenuously opposed Lesage's "Quiet Revolution," which aimed at increasing Quebec's independence from the federal union.

> Cast out the thousand
> prejudices where past
> encumbers present . . .
> struggle for the New Man.
> —PIERRE TRUDEAU
> in the first issue of Cité
> Libre, June 1950

cipal target of the magazine, but the Roman Catholic church also drew some fire. For example on one occasion Trudeau, himself a lifelong Catholic, sharply criticized the church's support for the government. "Some take the easy way out," he wrote, "by reiterating that authority comes from God. They omit to explain why God conferred it on a Stalin or a Hitler; or why, in our democracies, God would choose to express himself through the intermediary of electoral thugs or big campaign contributors."

There were other targets too, including Lester B. Pearson, who had succeeded Louis St. Laurent as leader of the federal Liberal party and as Canadian prime minister. At this time, Trudeau, Pelletier, and their friends leaned toward the moderately socialist New Democratic Party (NDP). They were openly antagonistic toward the Liberals, particularly on the issue of nuclear weapons. At the time, the United States was urging Canada to permit the stationing of Bomarc nuclear antiaircraft missiles on Canadian soil as part of the North American air defense system. With some reluctance, Pearson's Liberal government had agreed, drawing scorn from Trudeau in the pages of Cité Libre. Under the heading "The Abdication of the Spirit," Trudeau attacked the "cowardice" of the Liberals in accepting the missiles. "I have never seen," he wrote, "so degrading a spectacle as that of all these Liberals turning their coats in unison with their chief, when they saw a chance to take power." And then he went on: "The head of the troupe having shown the way, the rest followed with the elegance of animals heading for the trough."

Trudeau was particularly critical of Liberal members of Parliament (MPs) from his own province of Quebec. Too often, he argued, they simply voted blindly for whatever the Anglo-Canadian-dominated Liberal party leadership wanted. "The shameful incompetence of the average Liberal MP from Quebec," he wrote, "was a welcome asset to a government that needed little more than a herd of trained donkeys. . . . The party strategists had but to find an acceptable stablemaster—Wilfred Laurier, Ernest Lapointe, Louis St. Laurent—and the trained donkeys, sitting in the back benches, could be trusted to behave."

Few were safe from Trudeau's verbal lash. In a 1958 article entitled "Some Obstacles to Democracy in Quebec," Trudeau wrote: "Historically, French Canadians have not really believed in democracy for themselves; and English Canadians have not really wanted it for others. Such are the foundations upon which our two ethnic groups have absurdly pretended to be building democratic forms of government."

Trudeau left his government job in Ottawa in 1951. For the next few years, he continued to edit *Cité Libre*, allowing himself frequent time off for world travel. He went to Africa and to a communist economic conference in Moscow, fueling suspicions in some quarters that his sympathies were much more radical than he would admit.

Meanwhile, events were moving swiftly in Quebec. In 1959, Premier Duplessis had died suddenly. The

Demanding independence for Quebec, young demonstrators march through Montreal on Victoria Day, 1965. French-speaking separatists have long resented this legal Canadian holiday, which celebrates the birth of the British queen.

31

Trudeau (center) and Jean Marchand (right; b. 1918), hold a press conference in 1965 to discuss their decision to become Liberal candidates for Parliament. Known—along with Gérard Pelletier (b. 1919)—as Quebec's "Three Wise Men," the team was firmly opposed to the separation of Quebec from the rest of Canada.

blow to his party was magnified when his successor also died within a few months. The resulting uncertainty led to a victory at the polls for Quebec's Liberal party, led by a former federal cabinet minister, Jean Lesage.

Trudeau was enthusiastic about some actions of Quebec's new Liberal regime, which was moving to break the hold of the church over education and to enact broad social welfare measures. At the same time, he was distressed about Lesage's so-called Quiet Revolution, an effort to emphasize Quebec's nationalistic feelings. The Liberals' slogan for the 1962 provincial election, *"Maîtres chez nous"* ("Masters in our own house"), struck Trudeau as catering to the narrowest of nationalistic instincts while ignoring the reality of 20th-century economic facts. Trudeau was—and continued to be—a staunch advocate of Canadian unity, and a fierce opponent of all efforts to strengthen the nation's individual provinces.

Trudeau and his friends Gérard Pelletier and Jean Marchand were becoming increasingly well known for their outspoken comments on political matters. In 1965, they joined the Liberal party, announcing that they planned to reform it from within. The trio were soon the most famous French Canadians in the party. They came to be known as Quebec's "Three Wise Men."

Meanwhile, Prime Minister Lester Pearson was becoming deeply concerned about Quebec's growing promotion of French-Canadian nationalism. Pearson's advisers suggested that the "Three Wise Men" might give the federal government added strength in its conflict with Quebec. Of the three, Trudeau was the least attractive to Pearson. His trip to the communist conference in Moscow and his repeated attacks on the Liberals' nuclear policies made him anything but a welcome recruit.

But as Quebec's continued demands for special status for the province brought it ever more at odds with the federal government, the recruiting of the "Wise Men" became urgent. Pearson finally offered Marchand a cabinet post. Marchand said he would not join the Ottawa government unless Trudeau and Pelletier were brought along as well. Pearson, whose political worries also included the onset of terrorism attributed to an extremist group known as the *Front de Libération du Québec* (FLQ), had little choice but to accept Marchand's ultimatum.

Accordingly, Trudeau, Pelletier, and Marchand agreed to run for seats in Parliament, necessary prerequisites for positions in the cabinet. "Safe" election districts were found, and on November 8, 1965, all three were easily elected. Trudeau became MP for the Montreal district of Mount Royal.

Symbolizing the deep hostility of many French Canadians toward the British, a statue of Britain's Queen Victoria lies beheaded by a bomb in Quebec City. Police attributed the blast to separatist terrorists, whose acts of violence began to increase in the mid-1960s.

3

Apprenticeship to Power

Trudeau's critics charged him with hypocrisy for joining a government of which he had been so critical. He did indeed differ greatly with the federal Liberals on such matters as nuclear weapons. However, on the subject he considered most important for Canada—safeguarding the supremacy of the federal government while guaranteeing equal opportunity for its French-speaking citizens—Trudeau was in close alignment with Pearson's party.

When Trudeau arrived in Ottawa in 1965, the Canadian media quickly discovered it had an interesting character on its hands. Trudeau's individualistic lifestyle, his snappy Mercedes sports car, and his arrival for important meetings dressed in muddy corduroy slacks and a sports shirt shook the sober Canadian political world and caught the imagination of the normally straitlaced Canadian public.

Trudeau's often whimsical behavior seemed to suggest that he was an innocent adrift in the stern world of politics. This was far from being the case. After all, he had worked at the center of the Ottawa

Gérard Pelletier eases his way through a crowd on Ottawa's Parliament Hill. Pelletier, whom Trudeau once called "a moral authority of the highest importance, and my friend," served as secretary of state in Trudeau's cabinet, and later as Canada's ambassador to France.

Trudeau in 1965. When the "Three Wise Men"—Trudeau, Marchand, and Pelletier—arrived in Ottawa, the Canadian capital, most observers expected Marchand to be the trio's outstanding member; Trudeau's political flair and dashing personality, however, made him an instant national celebrity.

PUBLIC ARCHIVES CANADA

power structure in the Privy Council Office, and, as Pelletier observed, it was Trudeau who showed the other "Wise Men" how things worked in the federal capital.

But in the beginning, Marchand was considered the most politically promising of the three newcomers. In December 1965 he was named minister of citizenship and immigration in the federal cabinet. It was an important position in the government of a nation that, like the United States, had welcomed millions of refugees from overseas.

An important appointment for Pierre Trudeau, however, soon followed. In January 1966 he was named parliamentary secretary to Prime Minister Pearson. A Canadian parliamentary secretary has greater access than ordinary members of Parliament to information about government departments and about how the government functions. The position is generally regarded as a stepping-stone to higher office.

There is some hope that in advanced societies, the glue of nationalism will become as obsolete as the divine right of kings.
—PIERRE TRUDEAU
June 1964

There were some in Ottawa who were surprised at Trudeau's rapid advancement. Pearson, now enthusiastic about his former adversary, explained: "I had read his pieces for years, and was impressed by them, particularly by his detailed technical knowledge of economics and constitutional law. We're into a period where that's very important, and we'll be dealing a lot with Quebec. Pierre is a Quebecer, and seems to be the kind of qualified person we need."

Pearson's concern about relations with Quebec was centered on the growing demands from the provincial government for greater independence from the federal government. This movement toward autonomy had deep roots in the nation's history. Canadian settlement had been pioneered by France, which had sent 60,000 immigrants to the colony in the 17th and 18th centuries. The British had conquered Canada in 1759, but they had permitted Quebec's French-speaking residents to retain their language, their Catholic religion, and their French system of civil law. After the British conquest, however, Canada was flooded with English immigrants, who came to dominate the colony's government, business, and culture. When Canada became an independent country within the British Empire in 1867, French was once again legally recognized as the official language, along with English, of Quebec.

Long a largely agricultural society, Quebec had undergone a vast change in the mid-20th century. By the 1960s, it had become a heavily industrialized commercial center. Many of the province's 5 million French-speaking citizens, never comfortable with their minority status in the huge nation, now began to feel that their culture and economic survival were in danger of being overwhelmed by the nation's English-speaking majority, which outnumbered them by three to one.

Autograph-seekers surround Trudeau in London, England. The Canadian leader's breezy speech, well-publicized bachelor lifestyle, and unconventional approach to politics drew admiring crowds all over the world.

British General James Wolfe (1727–59) lies mortally wounded near Quebec on September 13, 1759. His forces outnumbered, Wolfe had vanquished the astonished French defenders before succumbing to the wounds he received in the battle. The fall of Quebec heralded the British conquest of Canada.

Reflecting these popular sentiments, the Quebec government began to strengthen its ties to other French-speaking governments abroad, acting in a way that suggested to many in Ottawa that Quebec was moving toward secession from the Canadian federation. This tendency met a quick response, particularly from the government of French president Charles de Gaulle. For him, Quebec presented a unique gateway to the technology of the North American continent quite apart from the province's ethnic and linguistic considerations, which were naturally of great importance to him. During a 1967 visit to Quebec, de Gaulle shouted *"Vive le Québec libre!"* (Long live free Quebec) at an official ceremony. The Quebecers cheered, but Pearson made it clear to de Gaulle that such sentiments were un-

welcome to the Canadian government.

Trudeau's performance as parliamentary secretary during the following year convinced Pearson he had been right in his assessment. On April 4, 1967, he elevated Trudeau to cabinet status by naming him federal minister of justice.

Trudeau's lack of regard for convention, his stylish clothes, and his reputation as an intellectual but glamorous man-about-town had already piqued Canada's curiosity. Followed by crowds of admiring teenagers, often photographed in fashionable spots in the company of attractive women, he was now a familiar figure on the national scene. His image as a politician, however, was not firmly established until, as minister of justice, he introduced legislation to reform Canada's divorce laws and Criminal Code.

Obtaining a divorce had never been easy in Canada. And, in the past, neither of the nation's two principal religious groups—the predominantly French Roman Catholics and the conservative English and Scottish Protestants—appeared eager to simplify divorce procedures. But pressure for change had been increasing, partly because of the influence of Canada's powerful southern neighbor. Canadians watched American movies and TV programs, read American magazines and books, listened to American popular music. America's relaxation of tough divorce laws and its rising divorce rate were beginning to make many Canadians feel their own country's laws were behind the times.

Trudeau's handling of the touchy divorce legislation won applause from almost all sides. His thoughtful explanations of the need for change were unusual coming from a federal cabinet minister, especially one who was a practicing Roman Catholic. Intellectual, legalistic, and impassioned by turns, he argued forcefully that "intolerable" physical and mental cruelty was, as well as adultery, a reasonable ground for divorce. "In a society which has moved so quickly and so far" in the 97 years since Canada's divorce laws had been written, he said, "it is not astonishing that the present divorce laws . . . are highly unsatisfactory and indeed produce some very evil results." He did not believe, he

Justice Minister Pierre Elliott Trudeau is rapidly emerging as the most exciting, lucid, and perhaps fearless of the candidates who will be seeking the national Liberal leadership.
—editorial in *The Telegram*
Toronto, Jan. 30, 1968

Separatist demonstrators clash with police during the tour of the Centennial Train in 1967. The railway exhibit, expected to promote national unity on the anniversary of Canada's confederation, ignited many such skirmishes as it moved through Quebec.

added, that the government was "entitled to impose the concepts which belong to a sacred society upon a civil or profane society." Trudeau's arguments touched a sympathetic chord in many Canadians.

They were similarly impressed by Trudeau's proposal to reform the Criminal Code. Many of its laws, he pointed out, were antiquated and almost impossible to enforce. Among them were laws dealing with such inflammatory topics as abortion, prostitution, and homosexuality. Many Canadians agreed with Trudeau's simple explanation of the need for new legislation: "The state," he said, "has no place in the nation's bedrooms."

This directness, however, also had a less pleasant side. Trudeau had always found it difficult to tolerate criticism or questions from those he considered less intellectually gifted than himself. It was during this period of his career that he frequently made headlines for dismissing critical comments indelicately, sometimes with vulgarity.

Shouting *"Vive le Québec! Vive le Québec libre!"* French president Charles de Gaulle (1890–1970) appeals to French-Canadian separatists from the balcony of Montreal's city hall on July 23, 1967. The French leader's performance infuriated many non-French-speaking Canadians.

But his overall performance as minister of justice had brought him to unusual prominence in the Ottawa establishment. When Pearson announced at the end of 1967 that he planned to retire as prime minister, Trudeau was naturally among those mentioned as possible successors.

Canada's Liberal party has traditionally alternated its leaders between French-speakers and English-speakers. Pearson, an English-speaker, had been preceded by St. Laurent, a French-speaker. That meant that, barring an unexpected development, Pearson's successor would be French-speaking. In addition, Canada had been swept by a tide of nationalistic fervor aroused by the celebration of its first centennial of nationhood. Montreal had staged a brilliant world's fair, called Expo '67, and for the first time Canadians began to have a strong sense of modern national identity. No longer would Canada be content with its role as a quiet neighbor

Multi-angled pavilions jut from the fairgrounds of Expo '67 in Montreal. The unprecedented success of the world's fair created a strong sense of unity and national pride among Canadians.

Justice Minister Pierre Trudeau prepares to enter Parliament's House of Commons before a 1967 hearing on the revision of Canadian divorce laws. Trudeau's cool, reasoned handling of this delicate issue gave his political career a significant boost.

of the United States or as the shy offspring of British and French cultures. The influx of new people from southern Europe, Asia, and the Caribbean, as well as the prosperity of the time, had led Canadians to feel that the whole world was opening up to them. The omens seemed good for Pierre Trudeau.

4

Into the Leadership

With Lester Pearson's announcement on December 14, 1967, that he would step down, the contest for the succession to the Liberal party leadership was thrown wide open.

Among the strongest candidates was Trudeau's friend Jean Marchand, still widely regarded as Quebec's senior statesman. Trudeau himself thought Marchand should seek the party leadership. But Marchand, outspoken and courageous though he was, felt he lacked the characteristics necessary to play the demanding public role of party leader and prime minister.

Trudeau, in the meantime, went off for a vacation in Tahiti. During his two weeks on the exotic Pacific island, he met a young woman from British Columbia, Margaret Sinclair, the daughter of a former Liberal cabinet minister. She would later become Trudeau's wife.

Trudeau returned from the Pacific to find that Marchand had taken himself out of the leadership race and that pressure was increasing for Trudeau to enter the contest. Leading the Trudeau supporters was Pearson himself. Soon after Trudeau returned to Ottawa, Pearson summoned him and

CANAPRESS PHOTO SERVICE

As the balloting for party leader at the 1968 Liberal convention finally draws to a close, Trudeau acknowledges the cheers of his followers with a triumphant salute.

Coolly nibbling on a carnation, Trudeau surveys the pandemonium surrounding him at the 1968 Liberal party leadership convention. He retained his attitude of skeptical amusement throughout the seven hours of voting that culminated in his election as party leader.

CANAPRESS PHOTO SERVICE

Marchand to his private office. He made it clear that if Marchand would not run, then Trudeau must.

Trudeau was still doubtful about entering the contest. He was afraid that if he made the race he would be thoroughly beaten by better-organized party professionals. If the defeat were severe, he believed, all the influence he had gained so far would be dissipated.

Offsetting what Trudeau felt was his lack of political expertise, however, was the intense publicity he was receiving from the media. In January 1968 Pearson sent Trudeau to all the provincial capitals to represent him in a dialogue about proposed constitutional changes. The trip put Trudeau's face on Canada's TV screens almost every night, as did his participation in a February constitutional conference. The public was already familiar with the political newcomer surrounded by squealing fans, and with the parliamentary debater presenting reform laws. Now they saw a tough and eloquent defender of Canadian unity. Pitted against Quebec's fiery separatist premier, Daniel Johnson, Trudeau proclaimed that the homeland of the French-Canadian population was all Canada, not just Quebec. He delivered a stirring plea for equal treatment for all the nation's citizens, both French- and English-speaking, and he emphatically stressed the need for strong provinces with equal rights under a united federal government. Trudeau's reputation as a political dilettante vanished overnight.

Finally, on February 16, 1968, he publicly announced his candidacy. In typical Trudeau fashion, he won further popular appeal with a self-deprecating appraisal of his chances. Talking with reporters after the announcement, he gave the following answer to a question about how he thought his entry into the race had occurred: "To be quite frank, if I try to analyze it, well, I think in the subconscious mind of the press it started out like a huge practical joke on the Liberal party."

Others, especially his critics, thought along the same lines. One, for example, wrote that Trudeau had "not so much run for public office, but had it thrust upon him."

If we win with him, will he be a good prime minister or will he be a dictator? He's so cool. No brush-offs. No impatience I can notice. The guy is a superman!
—PHILIP GIVENS
mayor of Toronto

Trudeau (left) and Prime Minister Lester Pearson confer during the constitutional conference of February 1968. Trudeau's national political stature was greatly increased by his eloquent call for a federal bill of rights to protect all Canadians.

It's not merely a revolt against the traditional style of politics; it is also a revolt against politics itself.
—DOUGLAS FISHER
Canadian journalist, on Trudeau's approach to politics

Newly elected leader of Canada's Liberal party, Trudeau is greeted with a roar of approval from the convention floor on April 6, 1968. The crowd, wildly excited by Trudeau's fourth-ballot victory, filled the hall with shouts of "Trudeau, Canada! Trudeau, Canada!"

UPI/BETTMANN NEWSPHOTOS

Flanking a beaming Prime Minister Pierre Trudeau (third from left), members of Canada's new administration head for their inaugural ceremonies at Ottawa's Government House on April 19, 1968. At far left is John Turner (b. 1929), Trudeau's finance minister; Jean Marchand is at far right.

Although by now committed to running for Canada's highest office, Trudeau persisted in alarming his political allies with his flippancy. In Toronto, for example, he was asked how badly he wanted to become prime minister. He smiled. "Not very badly," he said.

This was not entirely true. As the campaign wore on, Trudeau became ever more involved in its intricacies and gradually came to realize that, for many Canadians, both English- and French-speaking, the implementation of the ideas he espoused was seen as almost a last hope for preserving the Canadian confederation. His jokes and pranks continued, but the serious aspects of the campaign took on greater significance.

The Liberals met in Ottawa to choose their new leader on April 6, 1968. There were nine candidates, all prominent federal politicians. Trudeau led on the first ballot, but not by enough votes to win. One by one, the other candidates dropped out of the race, several of them throwing key support to Trudeau. It was still not enough, even after the third vote, for him to win. As the tension increased in the cavernous hall, filled with chanting supporters of the various contenders, Trudeau remained aloof. For over seven hours he stayed in his seat, occasionally playing to the cameras by tossing grapes in the air and catching them in his mouth. Finally, on the fourth ballot, he was declared the winner.

The Canadian Liberal party had a new leader and the country would have a new prime minister—Pierre Elliott Trudeau, so recently a carefree nomad, swimming the Bosporus, getting caught up in foreign civil wars, and buzzing around Montreal on a motorcycle. Neither Canada nor the party knew quite what to expect.

Trudeau motorcycles across a Northwest Territories airstrip in 1968. Canadians were intrigued with their 15th prime minister, but they were not quite sure what they had elected. Was he an adventurer, an intellectual, a playboy, a philosopher, a statesman—or, perhaps, a bit of each?

5

The First Taste of Power

Trudeau was sworn in as Canada's 15th prime minister on April 19, 1968.

His new position entitled him to live in the prime minister's official residence, 24 Sussex Drive, a sprawling mansion in a scenic and exclusive part of Ottawa. It was characteristic of Trudeau that he moved in with just two suitcases, which he carried himself.

He also brought with him the decisions he had made about the shape of his government and about how it should perform. The first task was to form a cabinet. That done, Trudeau called his first election as prime minister.

Under the Canadian system of government, the prime minister is the leader of the party that has the most members (MPs) in Parliament's House of Commons, the Canadian lawmaking body similiar to the U.S. Congress (Parliament's other body, the Senate, holds little real power). Elections for MPs must be held within five years of the previous election. However, the prime minister may dissolve the House and call for earlier elections if he or she chooses to do so.

Trudeau, occupying his new desk in the office of Canada's prime minister, jokes with reporters. One of his first official acts was to call an election for June 25, 1968.

Trudeau dances away the time while his campaign bus undergoes emergency repairs in June 1968. Such impromptu displays of high spirits delighted Canada's voters, who mobbed him wherever he appeared.

When Trudeau succeeded Pearson as leader of the Liberal party—and, therefore, as prime minister—his party had more seats in the House than any other, but it did not have a majority. To govern most effectively, a prime minister needs a majority in the House. Trudeau, hoping to get more members of his own party in the House, and wishing to receive a direct mandate from Canada's voters, called for new elections in June 1968.

The campaign was an even more wide-ranging, intense, and flamboyant affair than the campaign for the Liberal party leadership. Everywhere Pierre Trudeau went, he was mobbed by adoring fans. "Trudeaumania" reached its giddiest heights. The new prime minister, of course, helped fuel these fires of adulation. Every time he kissed a pretty girl, every time he delicately sniffed a flower, every time he jackknifed off a motel diving board, he had millions of observers. Television and newspaper cameras recorded every dizzy moment. Asked for her explanation of Trudeau's appeal, pop psychologist Joyce Brothers said he had "machismo," which she defined as "forcefulness and daring in a man."

But Trudeau also demonstrated that behind this freewheeling public persona there lay a much sterner person. This was most evident whenever Trudeau came face-to-face with the issue of Quebec separatism.

For example, late in the campaign, just after the assassination of Senator Robert Kennedy in the United States, Trudeau was speaking in a small city in Quebec. The crowd included a number of angry, shouting separatists. Trudeau endured the heckling for some time, but finally his temper erupted. "The men who killed Kennedy," he shouted, "are purveyors of hate like you—those who refuse to discuss. There won't be free speech in your 'Québec libre,' monsieur."

Throughout the province of Quebec, the tide of separatist feeling was rising. It reached a high point on June 24, 1968, the day celebrating French Canada's patron saint, John the Baptist. Before the holiday parade, Trudeau had given a moving speech before a crowd in St. Hyacinthe; he had stressed the

Since he was sworn in four weeks ago today, he has formed a government, built an admittedly temporary cabinet, dissolved Parliament, called a general election, put his party's electoral machinery in high gear, received his first state visitor, signed countless autographs, kissed any number of ecstatic women, made prime ministerial visits to Vancouver, Whitehorse and Edmonton and made a strongly political speech in Montreal.
—*The Telegram*
Ottawa, May 18, 1968

A shopkeeper displays samples of the Trudeau-inspired paraphernalia that flooded Canada in 1968. The phenomenon known as "Trudeaumania" included mobs of squealing teenagers, an avalanche of newspaper photographs and gossip items, and mountains of jewelry, T-shirts, and hats bearing the likeness of the nation's new prime minister.

need for national unity and the compatibility of bilingualism (the official use of both French and English) and Canadian identity. A large, restless crowd showed up for the parade festivities. Trudeau and other dignitaries took their places in the reviewing stand. Demonstrators had already made their presence known—distributing separatist leaflets and chanting the familiar *"Québec aux Québécois!"* (Quebec to the Quebecers). The arrival of the state officials only intensified the crowd's hostility, and it soon became violent. Pop bottles and other missiles were hurled at the police, who, outnumbered, were finding it difficult to maintain order. Some

Trudeau lashes out at hecklers in Quebec during the June 1968 campaign. Although he was generally easy-going and optimistic in public, Trudeau responded to separatists' taunts with furious indignation.

protesters wielded bats and even crowbars, and the separatists' chants became louder and louder. Trudeau approached the podium to deliver the short speech he had planned. Unable to be heard in the chaotic roar, he simply faced the crowd, refusing to leave or to duck the barrage of flying bottles. Impressed by Trudeau's courage, reporters in the press box put their notebooks down and, ignoring their own unwritten rule, rose to applaud. Trudeau was clearly gaining support with every separatist bottle that missed him.

Trudeau had decided to meet the separatist issue head-on. He was unwittingly assisted by the actions of the French government, which was becoming increasingly involved in Canadian political affairs. When France invited the Quebec provincial government—rather than the federal government in Ottawa—to attend a meeting of French-speaking countries in the African nation of Gabon, it was taken as a direct insult to the national regime. Trudeau dared Daniel Johnson, Quebec's premier, to accept the invitation, threatening to make it an issue in the election campaign. Johnson could read the political signs as well as anyone and knew that he would suffer a humiliating defeat in Quebec if he directly defied Trudeau at that time.

English-speaking Canadians were not alone in their enthusiastic approval of this lively new prime minister, who seemed so adept at "standing up to Quebec." There was also great admiration in Quebec for this intelligent, attractive son of their own province. That sentiment was heightened by the Quebecers' perception that, whereas in the past Quebec-born federal leaders had often been little more than tools of the Anglo-Canadian establishment, Trudeau was his own man. For the first time, a Quebec politician had co-opted the power base in Ottawa rather than being co-opted by it himself.

There were two strains running through the Trudeau campaign. One centered on the vision of the "flower child," the innocent intellectual who could sit sniffing a daisy while children tumbled around him. The other emphasized the image of the tough, brilliant politician who could and would defend

> *The nationalists—even those of the left—are politically reactionary because in attaching such importance to the idea of the nation they are surely led to the definition of the common good as a function of the ethnic group, rather than all the people.*
> —PIERRE TRUDEAU

Canada's integrity against all attacks, from without and within. Trudeau touched off an explosion of patriotism, a new feeling among Canadians that their country—rich but not opulent, not large in population but not insignificant either, friendly toward the United States but not simply in its shadow—had a unique role to play in the family of nations. It was this attitude that Trudeau addressed in one typical speech.

"Some people despair because they fear the future may escape us," he said. "But I speak to those who know that the future cannot be guaranteed to any person, province, or country—and the future will be what we make of it. It is up to us to know what to

Montreal police warily oversee the dispersal of stragglers on St. John the Baptist Day in 1968. Rioters had earlier pelted dignitaries reviewing the day's festivities with bottles and other missiles. Trudeau had faced the barrage unflinchingly, deeply impressing most onlookers.

CANAPRESS PHOTO SERVICE

do with this country we love."

The outcome of the election was never in doubt. Trudeau's opponent, Conservative leader Robert Stanfield, was a withdrawn and solemn Nova Scotia businessman whose cautious and colorless campaign was eclipsed by the glittering Trudeau bandwagon. When the votes were counted on June 25, 1968, Trudeau's Liberals had 155 of the 264 seats in the House of Commons. For the first time in 10 years, Canada had a government with a clear majority in Parliament. The main opposition to the Liberals would come from the Conservatives, who held just 72 seats. Pierre Trudeau had won by the largest electoral margin in Canadian history.

Conservative leader Robert Stanfield (b. 1914), was highly respected, but he lacked even a trace of the glamour that made his opponent unbeatable in the 1968 election. His campaign for the prime ministership was swamped by a tidal wave of enthusiasm for the charismatic Pierre Trudeau.

60

CANAPRESS PHOTO SERVICE

An optimistic Pierre Trudeau enters Liberal party headquarters in Ottawa to listen to election results on June 25, 1968. He was to learn that his party had recaptured control of Parliament by the largest electoral margin in Canadian history.

61

6

The Separatism Threat

With his new mandate, Trudeau set about establishing the "Just Society" he had promised during the campaign. He enlarged the number of people and departments responsible to the prime minister's office, in the process bringing a wave of young people and intellectuals into the government. Typical of the programs developed by this battalion of eager young bureaucrats was a project called Opportunities for Youth. OFY, which was roughly parallel in structure to the American Vista program, was intended to channel the energies of Canada's young people into projects that would benefit the nation as a whole. Members ran day-care centers for children, tended to the blind, charted wilderness trails, cleaned up public areas, even restored old cemeteries. "The government," said Trudeau, "believes that youth is sincere in its efforts to improve society. We intend to challenge them . . . to follow through on their criticism and advice." OFY was extremely popular until budget cuts forced its termination in 1975.

Trudeau's new government also made sweeping changes in Canada's foreign policy. Aimed at loosening the nation's tight bonds with the United

UPI/BETTMANN NEWSPHOTOS

Trudeau strengthens his bond with Canada's youth by meeting with former Beatle John Lennon (1940—80) and his wife Yoko Ono (b. 1933) in 1969. After their talk, Lennon said, "If all politicians were like Mr. Trudeau, then there would be world peace."

Securely established as prime minister after his landslide 1968 victory, Trudeau prepared to put his own stamp on Canada's government. Essential to his plans was the introduction of political newcomers to Ottawa—or, as he said during his campaign, "new guys with new ideas."

AP/WIDE WORLD PHOTOS

States and Europe, Trudeau reduced the size of Canada's military forces in the North Atlantic Treaty Organization, recognized the communist People's Republic of China, and began to phase out nuclear weapons.

Because Canada's political life was dominated by the increasingly strained relations between the English and French communities, bilingualism was high on Trudeau's list of priorities. He hoped to transform a set of provinces bitterly divided by language and cultural differences into "one united Canada"—a solid nation in which both French- and English-speakers would receive equal respect and equal opportunities to share in the nation's govern-

On their way home in October 1970, tanks of the 4th Canadian Mechanized Battle Group are loaded onto freight cars in West Germany. During his first term in office, Trudeau reduced Canada's NATO forces in Europe by one-half.

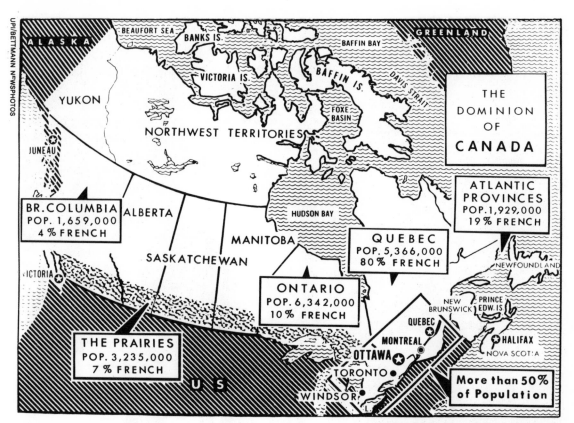

ALASKA

BEAUFORT SEA

BANKS IS.

BAFFIN BAY

GREENLAND

VICTORIA IS.

BAFFIN IS.

DAVIS STRAIT

YUKON

FOXE BASIN

NORTHWEST TERRITORIES

THE DOMINION OF CANADA

JUNEAU

BR. COLUMBIA
POP. 1,659,000
4% FRENCH

ALBERTA

HUDSON BAY

ATLANTIC PROVINCES
POP. 1,929,000
19% FRENCH

MANITOBA

SASKATCHEWAN

NEWFOUNDLAND

QUEBEC
POP. 5,366,000
80% FRENCH

VICTORIA

ONTARIO
POP. 6,342,000
10% FRENCH

NEW BRUNSWICK

PRINCE EDW. IS

THE PRAIRIES
POP. 3,235,000
7% FRENCH

QUEBEC

MONTREAL

HALIFAX

NOVA SCOTIA

OTTAWA

TORONTO

WINDSOR

U S

More than 50% of Population

ment and business life.

As a first step in this direction, Trudeau sponsored legislation aimed at improving the status of the French language in Canada. One of its provisions was a requirement that all federal civil servants (employees of the government) speak both French and English. This move was effective in relieving much intercultural tension, but it was highly unpopular in many English-speaking areas.

Despite Trudeau's efforts to reduce the discord between Canada's French and English factions, Quebec's estrangement from the rest of the country continued to grow. The potential secession of the province from the Canadian federation was posing an increasing threat.

Ever since the British conquest of Quebec in 1759, there had been rumblings of separatism throughout the former French colonies, not only in

A 1964 map of Canada shows the distribution of the nation's French- and English-speaking populations. When Trudeau was battling the movement to separate Quebec from the rest of Canada, one-third of the country's citizens considered themselves French Canadians.

A tense spectator watches experts dismantle one of the 17 bombs found in Montreal mailboxes on Friday, May 17, 1963. All the "Black Friday" bombs were thought to be the work of the *Front de Libération du Québec* (FLQ), the newly formed terrorist organization dedicated to securing Quebec's independence from Canada.

Quebec, where most of those of French descent lived, but also in the maritime provinces of Nova Scotia and New Brunswick, in parts of Ontario and, to the west, in Manitoba and Saskatchewan. Provincial dissatisfaction with federalism had sometimes broken out in open rebellion—in Quebec in 1837 and in the west in the last part of the 19th century. Separatism had also become entangled over the years with religious intolerance. Many Protestants bitterly opposed granting any special rights to French Canadians, most of whom were Roman Catholics. But, for the main part, the struggle to secure more equitable dealings for French-speaking Canadians was fought on a political level.

In the 1960s the separatist movement had grown slowly. It had been given an enormous amount of publicity, however, following President de Gaulle's 1967 visit, when he had uttered his famous *"Vive le Québec libre"* salute at Montreal's city hall. Many Quebec intellectuals and entertainers responded to de Gaulle's gesture with enthusiasm, some of them because they saw Paris as the only viable ally in the struggle to preserve Quebec's French culture against an English-speaking tidal wave.

Early in Trudeau's administration, ominous evidence began to indicate that Quebec's separatists were turning to more violent methods. At the vanguard of this new trend was the *Front de Libération du Québec*, the extremist separatist group that had been founded in 1963. The FLQ's objective was the violent overthrow of Canada's government, which it called a capitalist dictatorship run by the English-speaking Canadians and the United States. After the fall of the government, the FLQ proposed to make Quebec an independent Marxist nation.

At first the violence was limited to such acts as the dynamiting of federal mailboxes, and most Canadians dismissed it as the work of cranks. Even when terrorists bombed the Montreal stock exchange, injuring 27 people, few Canadians saw them as more than shadows on the political scene.

Then early on the morning of October 5, 1970, several "deliverymen" arrived at the Montreal home of James Cross, the British trade commissioner in

It was as if Canada had come of age, as if [Trudeau] himself single-handedly would catapult the country into the brilliant sunshine of the late 20th century from the stagnant swamp of traditionalism and mediocrity in which Canadian politics had been bogged down for years.
—the London *Spectator*
June 1968

The kidnapping of British diplomat James Cross (b. 1921) by FLQ terrorists sparked the "October Crisis" of 1970. This period of confrontation between the Canadian government and the FLQ posed a strong challenge to Trudeau's leadership abilities.

Quebec. Once they gained access to the house, they produced guns, overpowered Cross, bundled him into a taxi, and disappeared. Soon afterward, they identified themselves as members of the FLQ and demanded, for Cross's safe return, the release of 23 "political prisoners," $500,000 in gold, publication of a manifesto setting out their aims, and a plane to fly them to Cuba or Algeria. No longer was the FLQ to be taken lightly.

After Cross's kidnapping, Trudeau called a meeting of his cabinet to set out Ottawa's policy. The federal ministers, following a consultation with Quebec Premier Robert Bourassa, announced that Canada would not give in to the terrorists' demands, although they agreed to make some concessions. There was great anxiety for Cross's safety.

Four days after the kidnapping, the FLQ manifesto was broadcast on national radio and television

CANAPRESS PHOTO SERVICE

Pictures of "the patriot," the tough Quebec peasant who abandons his farm to challenge the government, were often seen during 1970's October Crisis. Quebec's symbol of militant independence, the image dates from the rebellion of 1837, when a ragtag band of farmers defeated an army of crack British soldiers.

and published in several newspapers. Government officials and many private citizens were outraged by the affair, but the public's reaction was mixed, especially in Quebec, where there was some sympathy for the FLQ, and a certain amount of amusement over the government's confusion. Nothing like this had ever happened in Canada before, and the government had clearly been caught off guard.

Soon, however, all doubts about the seriousness of the situation vanished. On October 10, Pierre Laporte, Quebec's minister of labor, was abducted from his Montreal home at gunpoint.

An Ottawa newsboy displays the headlines of October 16, 1970. The War Measures Act, invoked by the government after the FLQ kidnappings of British diplomat James Cross and Quebec Labor Minister Pierre Laporte, had never before been used in peacetime.

69

CANAPRESS PHOTO SERVICE

The faces of a Montreal couple reflect astonishment at the sight of armed soldiers at their doorstep. Thousands of troops patrolled Canada's normally tranquil streets during the October Crisis.

Both the Ottawa and Quebec governments immediately took measures to safeguard officials and official installations. Canadians were shocked to discover that armed soldiers were now patrolling their national capital. Some citizens were sufficiently alarmed at the sight to voice protests or at least to question whether such actions were necessary. Trudeau dismissed them with a statement that was to haunt the rest of his political life. "There are a lot of bleeding hearts," he said, "who just don't like to see people with helmets and guns. All I can say is, go on and bleed, but it is more important to keep law and order in society than to be worried about weak-kneed people who don't like the looks of an army." Trudeau's "bleeding heart" phrase was endlessly quoted by critics eager to prove his lack of concern for civil liberties.

Indirect negotiations had been conducted between the authorities and the terrorists but no progress had been made. As various deadlines, set by both sides, passed without result, the mood in Ottawa, Montreal, and Quebec City, the provincial capital, grew increasingly somber. Pressure was mounting on the officials, particularly the Trudeau government, to bring the affair to a head. Finally, threatened by violent mass demonstrations and confrontations between factions for and against the FLQ, Quebec's Premier Bourassa asked the federal government to send in the army. Bourassa also requested Ottawa to invoke the War Measures Act, a statute that dated back to World War I and that had never before been used in peacetime. Just before dawn on the morning of October 16, the federal government invoked the act, which gave the police almost unlimited powers to search homes and buildings without court warrants, and to arrest and detain without bail citizens suspected of acting in opposition to the authorities. It was now a crime to organize or attend a political rally or to be a member of the FLQ. It was also a crime to speak in support of the FLQ or, technically, even to have possession of its manifesto. The streets of Montreal rang with the heavy boots of 2,500 paratroopers and squads from Canada's Royal 22nd Regiment, the famous Vandoos, named for the colloquial pronunciation of the regiment's number in French, *vingt-deux*.

Trudeau appeared on national television that night to try to reassure Canadians that liberty was not dead in their country. He asserted that the powers that had been temporarily given to the police were necessary for dealing with a real threat to the nation's security.

"I appeal to all Canadians," he said, "not to become so obsessed by what the government has done today that they forget the opening play in this vicious game. That play was taken by the revolutionaries; they chose to use bombing, murder, and kidnapping."

Martial law is preferable to civil war.
—PIERRE TRUDEAU

The nation was stunned. It was even more stunned when the police and the army began a series of mass arrests in Quebec. Anyone who was suspected of even sympathizing with the FLQ was rounded up. Altogether, 465 people were detained. To many people concerned about civil liberties, Canada had become a police state.

On October 18, 1970, Montreal police, responding to a telephone call from the FLQ, found Pierre Laporte's body. He had been strangled by his captors.

"The FLQ," said a shocked Pierre Trudeau on national television, "has sown the seeds of its own destruction." Canadians agreed. Public support of the terrorist group, even in Quebec, virtually disappeared. FLQ violence came to an end, and most of those imprisoned under the War Measures Act were released. (Sixty-two people were eventually

A Montreal police official makes a grisly discovery on October 17, 1970: the body of Quebec Labor Minister Pierre Laporte (1921–70), stuffed into the trunk of a car. Laporte was murdered by the FLQ two days after imposition of the War Measures Act, which made FLQ membership a crime.

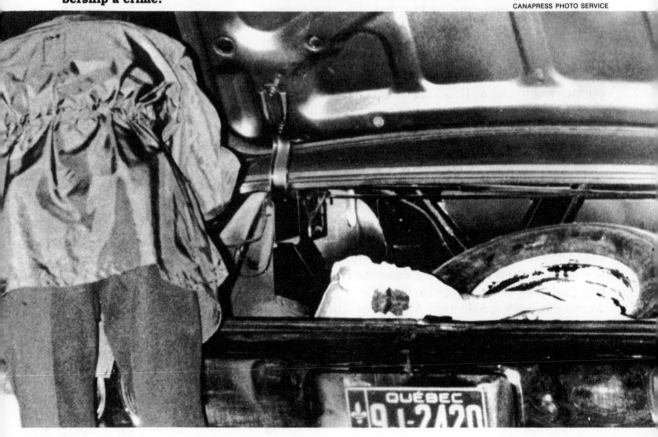

We have these men, having suspended the fundamental liberties of Canadians, revealing a total lack of concern for the use that the police forces of Quebec are making of their terrible power of discretion.

—*Le Devoir*
editorial on the War Measures Act, Montreal, Oct. 26, 1970

Lofting a defiant salute, FLQ terrorist Paul Rose enters a Montreal courtroom to stand trial for the murder of Pierre Laporte. Rose was found guilty and, in March 1971, he was sentenced to life imprisonment.

charged with a crime, and fewer than a dozen convicted.) In December, the government agreed to allow Cross's kidnappers to go to Cuba in return for the British official's release. Unharmed, Cross was freed on December 2. Laporte's killers were arrested on December 28. Tried and convicted, they drew long prison terms. The "October Crisis" was over.

7

The Fall from Favor

With the threat posed by the *Front de Libération du Québec* behind him, Pierre Trudeau was able to turn his attention to other matters.

On March 4, 1971, Trudeau, 51, was secretly married to 22-year-old Margaret Sinclair, the young woman he had first met in Tahiti. The marriage, which produced three sons, was to be a tempestuous one, probably in part because of the age difference between the two. It ended in divorce. The boys remained with their father after their parents separated.

By this time Trudeau's warm relationship with Canada's voters was beginning to cool. Early in his prime ministership, Trudeau had increased both the size and the power of the prime minister's personal staff. In previous regimes this staff had been relatively small and concerned primarily with a narrow range of duties directly concerned with the prime minister's routine functions. Trudeau's purpose in enlarging his staff's responsibility was to keep himself well informed and to make the government more efficient in its operations. His critics, however, accused him of placing too much power in the hands of his advisers, and of ignoring Par-

THE VANCOUVER SUN

Trudeau responds to a Vancouver heckler with a sample of the colorful—and sometimes obscene—language to which he often resorted in such situations. Celebrated for his witty and graceful speeches, the prime minister was also known for the ferocity of his attacks on opponents.

Supervised by his new bride and a priest, Pierre Trudeau signs the church registry after his March 1971 wedding in Vancouver, British Columbia. The Canadian public was delighted by their prime minister's marriage to the former Margaret Sinclair, but the union was to last for only six years.

liament, the officially elected representatives of the people. He was charged by some with being an "imperial prime minister"—of acting more like a king than the leader of a democracy. Instead of explaining and defending his style of leadership—which in practice was extremely effective—Trudeau impatiently brushed aside his critics, sometimes responding to questions in the House of Commons with a waspish comment or even an obscenity that gave his opponents further ammunition. On one notorious occasion Trudeau dismissed a critic with a distinctly un-prime-ministerial phrase. His remark was officially recorded as "fuddle duddle," a euphemism that became something of a catchword for such episodes. On another occasion, he said of the opposition members of Parliament: "When they get home, when they get out of Parliament, when they are 50 yards from Parliament Hill, they are no longer honorable members—they are just nobodies." Such comments did little to maintain Trudeau's earlier popularity.

His attitude toward members of the press was also often caustic. Before his marriage, for example, he had been highly annoyed by what he considered invasion of his privacy, especially when reporters tried to get details about his women friends. During a 1969 conference of commonwealth leaders, Trudeau learned that reporters had interviewed two women whom he had been dating. "Perhaps we had better have some files on all of you," he snapped to the newspeople, "and perhaps it would be useful if the police could go and question some of the women you have been seen with."

This tendency to bridle at press intrusiveness and at displays of political opposition antagonized voters in some key areas. Thus, on a trip through the Canadian west, Trudeau took great offense at some signs displayed by local wheat farmers. The placards, which protested Trudeau's apparent reluctance to try to increase foreign grain sales, were less than polite. Trudeau's response, however, was equally sharp. "If you want to meet me in the future," he said, "don't bring signs saying that Trudeau is a pig and don't bring signs saying that I

hustle women."

One well-known Canadian political writer, Peter C. Newman, took note of what he characterized as arrogance on Trudeau's part. When Trudeau had first come to prominence, Newman wrote that Canadians had been enthralled by Trudeau's "magic." But, said Newman, he had lost that touch, largely because of statements like the one he made when asked if he were going to call an election. "In God's good time," Trudeau had said, "whenever I feel it is best." Newman wrote about this attitude: "He was guilty of what the ancient Greeks called *hubris*, or overweening pride."

The upshot of all this was that by the time he called another election in the fall of 1972, much of his personal popularity had faded, particularly in areas outside of Quebec and Ontario.

The amendments to the Criminal Code and the

Visiting Mathura, India, in 1971, Trudeau receives a sacred mark on his forehead from a Hindu priest. The Canadian leader, always an enthusiastic traveler, had stopped in India on his way to a conference in the Southeast Asian republic of Singapore.

divorce laws, which had helped win Trudeau his first wide public acclaim, had been passed into law. And the Official Languages Act, one of the most significant pieces of legislation in Canada's modern history, had also become law. (This was a measure that guaranteed English- and French-speaking Canadians equality of opportunity and service in dealing with their government.) Despite Trudeau's activity in shepherding these—and many other—impressive legislative acts through Parliament, however, there was a feeling in much of the country that not much had really been accomplished.

Trudeau's popularity, surprisingly enough, was further decreased by his willingness to engage the voters in discussion and debate. During his first term of office, he had traveled across the country, speaking at countless meetings and conferences. His often biting replies to what he considered foolish questions at these functions antagonized not only the people directly addressed, but the wider audience as well. It was a case of familiarity breeding, perhaps not contempt, but certainly dislike.

To counter this trend, during the 1972 campaign Trudeau sought to stand above the immediate fray. The voters, however, wanted to express their unhappiness with what many of them considered to be Trudeau's mishandling of the economy. The facts seemed to reinforce their view. Unemployment had risen to its highest point in more than a decade. At the same time, inflation had also risen. Many of Canada's economic problems reflected conditions in the United States, where the effects of the Vietnam War were still causing turmoil in the economy. Many Canadians, however, thought that Trudeau's government had done too little to insulate the Canadian economy from foreign disarray. These critics felt that Trudeau was now insulting their intelligence by declining to campaign on the issues.

When the counting was over on October 30, Trudeau's Liberal party had won 109 seats in the House of Commons, the Conservatives under Robert Stanfield had 107, the socialist New Democratic Party (NDP) had 31, while minor parties and independents had 17.

It was always the acolytes, the hangers-on, the supposedly impartial observers who promised miracles from Canada's 15th prime minister. He himself promised little in concrete terms, which is just what he delivered.
—WALTER STEWART
Canadian historian

It appeared that the voters had delivered a stinging rebuke to Pierre Trudeau. There were even some members of his own party who said that he had lost his mandate and should resign as leader of the Liberals and thus resign as prime minister. But Trudeau refused to step aside. He insisted that the people had not repudiated the Liberals, but had expressed dissatisfaction with some of the party's policies. With that in mind, therefore, he would set about to change the policies forthwith.

The election results brought a deep change in Trudeau's attitude toward public affairs. During his first term in power, he had remained very much the intellectual, philosophizing about the rights and duties of governments and of the people being governed. Now he became a more practical, even cynical politician. He said about this time: "What kind of fools do governments have to be, not to say at election time, 'We'll give you lower taxes, higher old age pensions, price controls, everything you want'?"

A row of tractors, parked in front of Ottawa's Parliament Hill in 1968, symbolizes the unhappiness of Ontario corn raisers about falling prices. Trudeau's relationship with Canada's farmers deteriorated steadily during his first term in office.

Trudeau took his own advice. Policies requiring that a certain number of federal jobs be filled by employees who spoke both French and English were slowed down. That won approval in parts of Ontario and in western Canada. The traditional Canadian "open door" for immigrants was closed off slightly. That stifled resentment in areas of high unemployment, where the newcomers were often seen as unwelcome competitors for scarce jobs. A "total review" of the nation's social security system was begun. That pleased almost all working people.

During this period Trudeau's survival as prime minister depended to a great extent on not antagonizing the New Democratic Party which held the balance of power in Parliament. Therefore, when the worldwide oil crisis of 1973—74 resulted in a fourfold increase in prices for Canadian oil, Trudeau

Trudeau escorts an old friend, American singer Barbra Streisand (b. 1942), to a benefit at Ottawa's National Arts Center in 1972. The prime minister often scolded reporters for their curiosity about his personal life and his women acquaintances.

AP/WIDE WORLD PHOTOS

A future voter captures Trudeau's attention in Montreal. Hoping to improve his public image, Trudeau kept his contacts with the public to a minimum during his 1972 reelection campaign. His strategy, however, misfired: voters resented his unwillingness to debate such issues as unemployment and inflation.

was quick to follow NDP suggestions on ways to redesign Canadian oil policies and to protect Canadians from the rise in oil prices. The principal result was the formation of a state-owned oil company, eventually called Petro-Canada.

The net result of these actions was a return to popularity for Pierre Trudeau. The prime minister and his aides were not slow to notice the way the political winds were blowing. No longer were Liberal cabinet ministers so solicitous of New Democratic Party feelings. Trudeau himself seemed to go out of his way to dare the NDP to join with the Conservatives to defeat the Liberals in Parliament and so bring on another election. The NDP was not slow to take the dare, and on May 9, 1974, Trudeau's government was defeated on a confidence motion in the House of Commons. But Pierre Trudeau was unabashed. "I will return as prime minister," he declared.

It was a new Trudeau who undertook the election campaign. Where two years earlier he had been the distant statesman, now he was the cunning politician. Robert Stanfield, the Conservative leader, had provided the main topic for the campaign by advocating the imposition of wage and price controls. Sharply rising inflation caused by high oil prices had made Canadians, along with much of the industrial world, particularly anxious. But Trudeau poured scorn on the idea. He said it was quite unrealistic for Canada to try to isolate its economy from the rest of the world. He asked, sarcastically, if Stanfield could control Arab oil producers by saying, "Zap! You're frozen!"

It was a deadly thrust. And Trudeau hammered

A Canadian service-station attendant pumps gas under a new sign: Petro-Canada. The Trudeau government, making concessions to the socialist New Democratic Party, created the national oil company during the 1973–74 oil crisis.

CANAPRESS PHOTO SERVICE

it home relentlessly. Speaking with a new vigor and new humor at four or five rallies every day, he criss-crossed the country. There was a new feature to the campaign, too. Previously, Trudeau had insisted that his wife would not take part in politics. This time she joined heartily in the campaign; her diffident, youthful charm proved to be an enormous political asset.

On July 8, 1974, after the votes were counted, the Liberals had won a clear majority in Parliament. It seemed that Pierre Trudeau had learned the practical value of humility and in doing so had won back the support of the people. But the newly revived romance would prove to be of short duration.

Margaret and Pierre Trudeau greet supporters in Toronto before the 1974 national election. The public loved Margaret's speeches about her husband ("He's a beautiful guy," she would say), and Liberal party politicans appreciated her vote-getting power. Trudeau easily won reelection.

8

Into the Wilderness

The 1974 election campaign had brought a new view of Pierre Trudeau into the Canadian imagination. The quick pace of his campaign, the vigor and humor of his speeches, and the presence of his beautiful young wife gave rise to the public expectation that his new government would display the same liveliness. Canadians therefore were disappointed when that expectation was not realized. The new mandate to govern seemed to be dissipated in endless surveys and conferences and in tampering with the civil service and the passage of old and unimportant legislation. Where were the new directions? Where were the new ideas? Where was the new Trudeau?

Trudeau was puzzled by the apparent demand for action from the Canadian people.

"Do they want somebody on a white horse charging forth and saying 'You follow me,' or do they want to look at the results and ask themselves if this country by and large, given its advantages and problems, has done as well or better, or worse than most?"

Whatever Canadians wanted, at the moment it was evidently not Trudeau. In one public opinion

CANAPRESS PHOTO SERVICE

Finance Minister John Turner (b.1929) announces his resignation on September 11, 1975. The departure of Turner, the most popular member of Trudeau's cabinet, sent shock waves through the Liberal party. In the public mind, Trudeau alone was now responsible for the state of the economy—which was deteriorating rapidly.

Proving that not all Trudeau fans are teenagers, a vintage Montreal voter beams admiringly at the prime minister. Trudeau's popularity was at a peak after his energetic 1974 campaign, but it began to slide when his new administration failed to make the exciting moves voters had expected.

CANAPRESS PHOTO SERVICE

poll after another, Trudeau's personal popularity was shown to be eroding swiftly, and that of his government even faster.

The situation was aggravated by the continued poor state of the economy. Inflation was even more of a worry to the average Canadian than it had been

before the election. Pressure on the government to take decisive action was growing steadily throughout the summer of 1975. The public's confidence was further weakened by the resignation on September 11, 1975, of Finance Minister John Turner, who had been regarded by many inside and outside

Protesting Trudeau's program of wage and price controls, thousands of union members from all over Canada assemble on Ottawa's Parliament Hill in March 1976. The demonstration was one of many preceding the nationwide strike that paralyzed the country the following October.

the party as Trudeau's most likely successor.

For the next month, the country seemed to be sweeping relentlessly toward new economic perils. The federal cabinet debated various strategies for dealing with inflation, now made worse by declining productivity in Canada's farms and factories. Finally, on October 13, the evening of the Canadian Thanksgiving holiday, Trudeau went on national television to outline his course of action. Warning the country that it faced a program of economic restraints that would be "the heaviest since the Second World War," he announced the imposition of mandatory wage and price controls.

Businessmen and workers alike felt they had been cheated; that Trudeau had callously done the very thing he and they had laughed at Stanfield for even proposing. For much of the next year there were protests of various sorts, culminating in a massive strike action on October 14, 1976, when a million Canadian workers stayed away from work to protest the continued use of wage controls.

At about this time Trudeau's private life began to become very public. The behavior of Margaret Trudeau had first caused whispers during a 1976 trip to Latin America. Then came a highly publicized weekend party in Toronto with the Rolling Stones rock group and several uninhibited interviews in U.S. magazines. The Trudeaus separated in May 1977 and were eventually divorced.

There was political scandal too. Two Liberal cabinet ministers were accused of trying to influence a federal judge. A Liberal senator was found to have profited by dealings in shares of a company that won concessions at federal airports. The state-owned company Atomic Energy of Canada Ltd. was reported to have spent $10 million on questionable payments to political figures in Argentina and South Korea. Another Liberal cabinet minister was found to have sent his children's nursemaid home to Scotland in a Defense Department plane.

But most seriously, in 1977, came startling revelations about the activities of the Royal Canadian Mounted Police. The Mounties over the years had earned a reputation for relentless and honest police

> *Parliament—and indeed the government—has lost or is close to losing effective control of the public purse.*
>
> —JAMES MACDONNELL
> Canadian auditor general

Ottawa demonstrators express their anger over Trudeau's economic policies in March 1976. One of the marchers wears a mask lampooning Trudeau.

work, often in the most trying conditions. It was therefore a substantial shock for many Canadians when it was revealed that for years the Mounties had engaged in illegal surveillance of suspected members of the Quebec separatist movement. Illicit mail opening, arson, burglary, and illegal wiretapping were some of the offenses involved. Even in English-speaking Canada, where sympathy for the separatists was almost nonexistent, citizens were appalled by this evidence of government-sanctioned lawbreaking and disregard for civil liberties.

Dancing at a New York City discotheque, Margaret Trudeau personifies a lifestyle that many Canadians found somewhat shocking. After a number of highly publicized disagreements, Pierre and Margaret Trudeau separated in 1977.

As Britain's Queen Elizabeth II (b. 1926) leads other guests from a Buckingham Palace reception room, Pierre Trudeau breaks into a solo dance step. This 1977 photograph of the Canadian prime minister's departure from palace formality delighted people all over the world, particularly in Canada.

Meanwhile, another storm cloud had been developing in Quebec. This finally blossomed into a full-scale squall with the November 1976 election of René Lévesque and the *Parti Québécois*, a combination dedicated to achieving Quebec's independence from Canada.

Lévesque had promised to stage a referendum, or popular vote, on the first step toward independence, a stage he called "sovereignty-association." Under such an arrangement, Quebec would remain loosely linked to Canada in much the way that countries of the European Common Market are connected but would, for all practical purposes, be a sovereign nation. Once more, the rest of Canada looked to Trudeau to subdue a threat to national unity. Trudeau now demonstrated masterly political skill. He took a calm, conciliatory tone toward the potentially rebellious Quebecer, and refused to engage in direct confrontation with Lévesque. He talked of changing the constitution to guarantee that any citizen could be "at one and the same time, a good Canadian and a good Quebecer." He spoke of Quebec's separation as "a crime against the history of mankind," and of Canadians' "holy mother, the nation." Trudeau's approach succeeded; popular opinion in Quebec swung away from independence. Realizing that he could not win the referendum, Lévesque postponed it until a more favorable time.

Public opinion polls showed that Trudeau enjoyed a brief surge of popularity after his victory over Lévesque and the Quebec separatism referendum. Inflation, however, continued to rise, and the national mood was dark. Trudeau dismantled wage and price controls in the spring of 1978, but the move had little effect on Canada's troubled economy. Unemployment was on the increase and the budget deficit, at $11.5 billion, was the highest in Canada's history. Trudeau was not in the best of forms for the election due the following year.

After Conservative party leader Robert Stanfield's 1974 defeat and resignation, the Conservatives had elected a new leader. He was Joe Clark, a likable young politician from the western Canadian province of Alberta. Already a favorite of western voters,

A lot of Canadians don't think you understand them because you are privileged yourself, you are secure yourself. That's a very isolating thing for a hard time.

—BARBARA FRUM
journalist, interviewing
Trudeau on Oct. 13, 1976,
the first anniversary of the
imposition of wage and
price controls

Members of the Royal Canadian Mounted Police check their equipment in an Ottawa barracks. The Mounties' spotless reputation was stained in 1977, when official testimony revealed that, in its pursuit of suspected terrorists, the elite corps had regularly broken the law.

The newly elected premier of Quebec, René Lévesque (b. 1922), ponders a reporter's question during a November 1976 news conference. Lévesque and Trudeau, who represented opposite sides on the separatism issue, were political enemies for decades. As loyal French Canadians, however, they maintained a grudging mutual respect.

Clark was strengthened by Trudeau's tactless comments during the 1979 election campaign. "Farmers are professional complainers," he told a gathering in Quebec. "When there is too much sun, they complain. When there is too much rain, they complain. A farmer is a complainer."

The complaints were registered in the form of votes on May 22, 1979. Trudeau's regime was buried. Clark's Conservatives won 136 seats, just six short of a clear majority. The Liberals won only 114 seats and the NDP 26. The Liberals had taken their worst shellacking in the west. In 1968, they had won 26 seats in the four provinces west of Ontario; in 1979 they won three. There was considerable grumbling in the Liberal party about Trudeau's leadership. Some said he had strayed too far from the party's grass roots. Nevertheless, when he announced on November 21 that he was stepping down as leader of the party, a ripple of shock ran through the country. Canadians might not want Pierre Trudeau as prime minister, but they had grown used to having him around.

A leadership convention was planned for March 1980 to select his successor. Most Canadians believed that the Trudeau era was over at last.

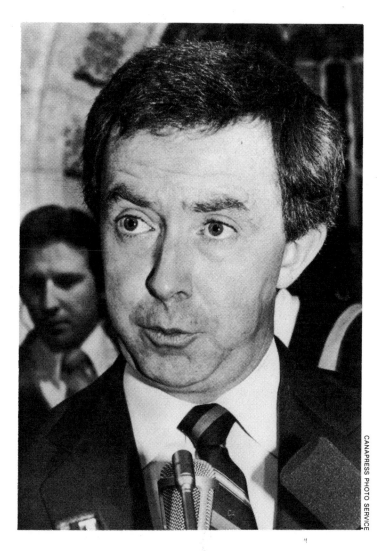

Joe Clark (b. 1939), the Conservative leader who displaced Trudeau as prime minister in 1979, established an efficient, no-nonsense administration. Forced to call an election soon after taking office, however, Clark discovered that Canadians preferred Trudeau's lively and unconventional style of governing to his own businesslike approach.

CANAPRESS PHOTO SERVICE

9

Return of the Prodigal

About six months after Clark's election, the Conservative government presented its first budget. Among its provisions was a substantial increase in taxes, including a hefty rise in the gasoline tax. It was an unpopular document, and it gave the Liberal party a chance to regain the political offensive. It also altered Pierre Trudeau's plans to retire from politics.

As the debate on the budget resolution began, a crisis atmosphere overtook Parliament Hill. Everyone knew that the Conservatives, lacking a clear majority in the House of Commons, were extremely vulnerable. The Liberals were determined to muster as much strength as possible, even pulling two of their members from their hospital beds for the crucial budget vote on the night of December 13. When the deciding vote was called, the NDP sided with the Liberals; the Conservative government was defeated by 139 votes to 133.

The next day, Parliament was officially dissolved and an election called for February 18, 1980. Joe Clark's Conservative government had lasted for less than seven months.

Pierre Trudeau faces the public with high-spirited confidence in 1980. Bored by their short exposure to Joe Clark, Canadians repaid Trudeau's optimism with a resounding majority of their votes.

CANAPRESS PHOTO SERVICE

CANAPRESS PHOTO SERVICE

Candidate Trudeau presents himself with open arms to a Nova Scotia rally. Soundly rejected by the voters less than a year earlier, Trudeau made a stunning comeback in 1980; he received almost the same percentage of the vote as he had won in the "Trudeaumania" election of 1968.

In the beginning, the advantage seemed to lie with the Conservatives. Three days after the election was called, Prime Minister Joe Clark, confident of being returned to office with a clear majority, was off on his campaign plane. By contrast, the Liberals, leaderless since Trudeau's resignation, were uncertain about their course of action. After a lengthy debate, in which arguments raged both for and against Trudeau's return to leadership, the party invited Tru-

deau to take back his old job. He accepted.

"It was not my desire to lead again," he said, "but my colleagues and myself saw it as my duty."

The 1980 election campaign was hardly a contest. Polls taken in December showed Trudeau 20 points ahead of Clark. Both sides, for the first time in Canada, used TV commercials to launch personal attacks on the other; the unsophisticated Clark—unkindly nicknamed "Joe Who?"—seemed, some-

Shouting separatist slogans, demonstrators march through Montreal on May 20, 1980, the day of the referendum on Quebec's independence. Trudeau's intensive campaign against the separatism measure paid off: it was rejected by three out of five Quebec voters.

An Ottawa crowd, angry about rising interest rates, prepares to hang an effigy of Trudeau in November 1981. Although he had won his latest battle against Quebec separatism, Trudeau still faced the difficulty of governing under worsening economic conditions.

how, easier to lampoon than the worldly, self-confident Trudeau. In the end, voters—already tired of Clark's somewhat colorless style, and eager for the return of the dashing and witty Trudeau—gave the Liberals a clear majority in the House of Commons. Acknowledging his cheering supporters at Liberal campaign headquarters, the broadly smiling victor opened his arms and said, "Welcome to the '80's!" Prime Minister Pierre Trudeau was back.

Early in his new term, Trudeau was once again confronted with his perennial opponent, Quebec Premier René Lévesque. On April 15, 1980, Lévesque announced that a referendum on Quebec's independence would be held on May 20. Quebecers would be asked to vote on whether or not they wished Lévesque's government to take the first steps toward separation from Canada.

Trudeau had little time to marshal his forces, but with characteristic single-mindedness, he did so. In his parliamentary "Throne Speech"—the formal address in which the government sets out its intentions for the coming session—Trudeau told the citizens of Quebec that, no matter how they voted, Lévesque could not deliver what he promised: a sovereign nation with economic ties to Canada. He told them that the premiers of the nine English-speaking provinces had given notice that they would never enter a common market with an independent Quebec. Such a nation, he pointed out, would be a tiny French island virtually lost in an English-speaking sea. Trudeau renewed his pledge to change the constitution in a way that would specifically guarantee the rights of French-speaking Canadians.

Speaking as a Quebecer himself, Trudeau made an impassioned speech in Quebec City just before the referendum. "It takes more courage," he said, "to stay in Canada and fight it out than to withdraw into our walls." Quebec listened. Almost 60 percent of the electorate voted against authorizing Lévesque to seek separation. "I have never been as proud to be a Quebecer and a Canadian," said Trudeau.

To many Canadian observers, this had been Pierre Trudeau's finest hour. He had been summoned to Ottawa by Lester Pearson as one of three "wise men" who could help keep Quebec in the Canadian federation and thus preserve the nation's integrity. Although there had been many ups and downs, especially in other areas of government activity, on this central issue Trudeau had never wavered. The same steely will he had displayed in the time of the FLQ crisis, although shown in a softer, more humane manner in the campaign leading up to the referendum, prevailed.

He controlled the political system absolutely, but he could not make it work.
—the *Globe and Mail* editorial on Trudeau's performance as prime minster, printed during the 1980 campaign

With the referendum safely over, Trudeau turned his attention to the constitutional reform that he had promised. In 1980, Canada actually had no constitution of its own. Its government functioned under the terms of the British North America (BNA) Act, legislation passed more than a century earlier by the British Parliament. The BNA Act had formally united the separate British colonies and territories to the north of the United States into one self-governing entity. The 1867 British North America Act gave the federal government extensive power over taxation, trade and commerce, military defense, navigation and shipping, banking and currency, marriage and divorce. The act gave the provincial governments control over the administration of local justice, education, municipal government, property, and civil rights.

From time to time there had been discussions of "patriating" the BNA Act, a process that would give Canada, rather than Britain, the right to amend the act. Largely because the individual provincial governments had never been able to agree on how amendments would be enacted, the BNA Act had remained unchanged.

Now Trudeau proposed that the BNA Act be patriated immediately, and that the resulting new constitution include a Canadian version of the U.S. Bill of Rights. Canada already had such a statute, but it was merely an act of Parliament, and could be changed at will by any other session of Parliament. Trudeau wanted it incorporated into the new constitution and therefore outside the authority of Parliament.

Trudeau's proposed charter of rights would include guarantees that both French and English would be used in the courts and legislatures of the provinces where both languages were widely spoken, and that schoolchildren in all provinces would be taught in whichever language local preference dictated.

It took a year of raging debates, political infighting, constant negotiating, and discreet maneuvering, but on November 5, 1981, Trudeau and all the provincial premiers—except Quebec's Lévesque—

Pierre Trudeau did one magnificent thing. . . . He created passion where there was dullness, elegance where there was drabness, spontaneity where there was artifice, mystique where there was ordinariness.
—the Victoria Times letter to the editor during the 1980 campaign

reached a compromise. They agreed to send the revised constitution to London for official approval by the British Parliament.

At one stage of the constitutional battle, Trudeau had hinted that he would step aside as prime minister after the negotiations had been concluded. The challenges of the drawn-out process, however, had noticeably revived his spirits. When, in December 1981, he was asked about his future, he said, "I'm governing now. I have no plans for retirement."

Trudeau and his sons in 1982. The boys (clockwise from upper left) are: Justin (b. 1972), Michel (b. 1975), and Sasha (b. 1974). Trudeau was always unusually close to his children. "When they were with him," notes one biographer, "he was an entirely different person: tender and joyous, as if not quite believing in his luck."

10

The Twilight's Glow

In 1982, on a rainy spring day on Parliament Hill, Britain's Queen Elizabeth II signed the proclamation that officially gave Canada a new constitution. The legislation had already been approved by the British Parliament. Thousands of Canadians defied the elements to witness and applaud the ceremony.

With that milestone behind him, Pierre Trudeau seemed to undergo yet another change in his relationship with the people of Canada. Although his travels had taken him from one end of the vast country to the other, his fellow Canadians remained something of a mystery to him.

In the summer of 1983, on a visit to southern Ontario, he mused about this. "There was acre upon acre of farmland, and all we could see—though I pressed my forehead against the cold window—all we could see were little lights here and there," he said of driving through the countryside. "And I was wondering, what kind of people live in those houses? And what kind of people worked in this part of Canada, and lived and loved here?

"I felt that my job, in a sense, is not all that different from the jobs that most of you have—those of you who have jobs, because I know there are those

UPI/BETTMANN NEWSPHOTOS

A pensive prime minister takes a break during sessions of the 1984 economic summit meeting in London. Trudeau became increasingly concerned about international affairs during his last term in office.

At an April 17, 1982, ceremony in Ottawa, Trudeau faces Britain's Queen Elizabeth II as he signs the proclamation giving Canada its own constitution. Of all his achievements, Trudeau was proudest of his part in creating this document.

UPI/BETTMANN NEWSPHOTOS

who are unemployed, too. It is to start work in the morning and work at things and hope to get them finished by 6 or 7, when you get home and see your family, and then often to work again after, as I know you do."

And as he pondered his relationship and his connection with the Canadian people, Trudeau was also beginning to wonder about the place he had established on a larger scene, as a world statesman.

It was at this time that he began to work vigorously to promote a dialogue among the world's nations. His mission was to diminish the threat of nuclear war, and to help to close the gap between rich and poor countries. Even among his friends his quest seemed quixotic, a sort of tilting at nuclear windmills. But Trudeau was committed. He set off on a series of far-ranging travels, visiting world leaders in Europe, India, Japan, China, the Soviet Union, and the United States. Publicly, in Washington, President Ronald Reagan endorsed Trudeau's ideas. Privately, however, a high Reagan aide called Trudeau an unrealistic dreamer. Konstantin

Trudeau greets Soviet leader Konstantin Chernenko (1911—85) at a Moscow reception in 1984. As his prime ministership drew to a close, Trudeau traveled extensively, campaigning for greater understanding among members of the world community.

CANAPRESS PHOTO SERVICE

Chernenko, then the Soviet leader, was polite but noncommittal.

Although Trudeau's mission had no immediate results, it won him a nomination for the Nobel Peace Prize. Trudeau himself believed the time he had spent on it had been worthwhile. On his return to Canada, he said: "Let it be said of Canada, and of Canadians, that we saw the crisis, that we did act, that we took risks, that we were loyal to our friends and open with our adversaries, that we lived up to our ideals and that we have done what we could to lift the shadow of war."

By now, Trudeau had decided it was time to leave the office of prime minister. His departure was widely expected in Canadian political circles, but there was some surprise that it had come so quickly and so quietly when it was announced on February 29—Leap Year Day 1984.

Although Trudeau remained an enigma to many

Visiting Washington, D.C., in 1983, Trudeau listens to President Ronald Reagan (b. 1911) praise his quest for international peace. Despite his public approval of Trudeau's mission, the American president was reported to be doubtful about its practicality.

A lone angler plies the waters of a lake in Jasper National Park, high in the Canadian Rocky Mountains. Canada's almost 4 million square miles include majestic mountains, ice-covered islands, rolling prairies, rich farmlands, and forest-edged seacoast bays, as well as densely populated, modern cities.

people during his nearly 20 years in public life, he was at times the most flamboyant and charismatic figure on the world scene. More an abstract than a practical thinker, as prime minister he nevertheless shrewdly executed major policies and effectively brought about significant changes almost single-handedly. Even his style of dress—which ranged from finely tailored Italian suits to leopard-print swim trunks—delivered a mixed message about his personality. A Canadian political observer, Jean-Paul Desbiens, wrote: "What is the paradox of Pierre Elliott Trudeau? It is to be a man who lives in liberty to the limit instead of whining about alienation. It is to adopt deliberately the comportment of an aristocrat among men who have contempt for superiority or even differences from the norm. It is to aim at reason rather than play on emotion."

More than 1 million people live in Montreal, one of Canada's most sophisticated and architecturally striking cities. A major port and rail center, Montreal contains 5 TV and 22 radio stations, 80 hospitals, 5 universities, and one of the world's most efficient subway systems.

ART RESOURCE

Framed by Canada's national symbol, a maple leaf, Prime Minister Trudeau makes his formal exit from politics at the Liberal leadership convention in June 1984. He had served as his country's top elected official for 16 years.

The reaction to Trudeau's departure was as varied as those who spoke of it. Former U.S. president Richard Nixon called him "one of the ablest leaders of the Western world." But the French-language newspaper *La Presse* said he had failed "to dissipate the sovereignist dream in Quebec or to conciliate English-speaking people in the West." Willy Brandt, ex-chancellor of West Germany, said history would remember Trudeau as "one of those remarkable personalities."

Perhaps the most colorful salute was paid in the House of Commons, where Trudeau had been the center of so many storms. A member from the western province of Alberta said: "After almost 16 years of riding tall in the saddle, our prime minister has decided to hang up his spurs. He leaves his footprints all over the nation."

It had been a long time since the day when, infuriated by what he regarded as a despotic Trudeau action, a socialist member of Parliament had pointed to the prime minister across the vaulted chamber of the House of Commons and shouted, "There, but for the grace of Pierre Elliott Trudeau, sits God!"

Pierre Trudeau alternately fascinated and infuriated Canadians, but he never bored them. Jaunty, charming, witty, resourceful, and intelligent, he could also be impatient, arrogant, and aloof. At his best, however, Trudeau personified the qualities his countrymen most admire: courage, independence, and unshakable integrity.

Further Reading

Brebner, J. B. *Canada: A Modern History*. Ann Arbor: University of Michigan Press, 1970.

Broadbent, Edward. *The Liberal Rip-off: Trudeauism vs. the Politics of Equality*. Toronto: New Press, 1970.

Butler, Rick and Jean-Guy Carrier, eds. *The Trudeau Decade*. Doubleday Canada Limited, 1979.

Cook, Ramsay. *Canada: A Modern Study*. Toronto: Clarke, Irwin & Co., 1977.

Cowley, Michael. *The Naked Prime Minister*. Winnipeg: Greywood Publishing, 1969.

Gwyn, Richard. *The Northern Magus*. Toronto: McClelland and Stewart, 1980.

Harbron, John D. *This is Trudeau*. Don Mills, Ontario: Longmans Canada Limited, 1968.

Laxer, James and Robert. *The Liberal Idea of Canada: Pierre Trudeau and the Question of Canada's Survival*. Toronto: Lorimer, 1977.

Malcolm, Andrew. *The Canadians*. New York: Times Books, 1985.

Radwanski, George. *Trudeau*. New York: Taplinger Publishing Company, 1978.

Stewart, Walter. *Trudeau in Power*. New York: Outerbridge & Dienstfrey, 1971.

Stuebing, Douglas. *Trudeau! A Man for Tomorrow*. Toronto: Clark, Irwin & Co., 1968.

Trudeau, Pierre Elliott. *Conversations with Canadians*. Toronto: University of Toronto Press, 1972.

———. *Pierre Elliott Trudeau: Portrait in Time*. Montreal: Stanké, 1977.

Westell, Anthony. *Paradox: Trudeau as Prime Minister*. Scarborough, Ontario: Prentice-Hall of Canada, 1972.

Chronology

Oct. 18, 1919	Joseph Pierre Yves Elliott Trudeau born in Montreal, Canada
1940	Graduates from Jean de Brébeuf College in Montreal
1943	Receives law degree from University of Montreal
1945	Graduates from Harvard University with master's degree in political economy
1946	Studies at the Sorbonne in Paris
1947	Studies at the London School of Economics under Harold Laski
1949	Works as lawyer for striking asbestos miners in Quebec
1950	Joins Privy Council Office in Ottawa First issue of *Cité Libre* magazine appears in June
Nov. 8, 1965	Elected to Parliament
April 4, 1967	Appointed federal minister of justice
April 1968	Elected Liberal party leader; becomes prime minister of Canada
June 25, 1968	As prime minister, gains huge victory in national elections
Oct. 1970	Invokes War Measures Act after a wave of separatist terrorism
March 4, 1971	Marries Margaret Sinclair
Oct. 30, 1972	Narrowly wins his second election as prime minister
July 8, 1974	Regains a clear parliamentary majority in new election
Oct. 13, 1975	Announces imposition of price and wage controls
May 22, 1979	Defeated in national elections by Conservative Joe Clark, who becomes prime minister
1980	Regains prime ministership in electoral victory over Clark; successfully campaigns for a "no" vote in referendum on Quebec's secession from Canada
1981	Secures approval of new Canadian constitution from nine of Canada's ten provincial premiers
1983	Embarks on a campaign to avert nuclear war
1984	Announces his retirement from politics on February 29 Leaves office in June

Index

Thomas Butson has been assistant news editor of *The New York Times* since 1968. A former assistant managing editor of *The Toronto Star*, he covered Pierre Trudeau's political emergence and rise to power. He is also the author of *Gorbachev* in the Chelsea House series WORLD LEADERS   PAST & PRESENT.

Arthur M. Schlesinger, jr., taught history at Harvard for many years and is currently Albert Schweitzer Professor of the Humanities at City University of New York. He is the author of numerous highly praised works in American history and has twice been awarded the Pulitzer Prize. He served in the White House as special assistant to Presidents Kennedy and Johnson.